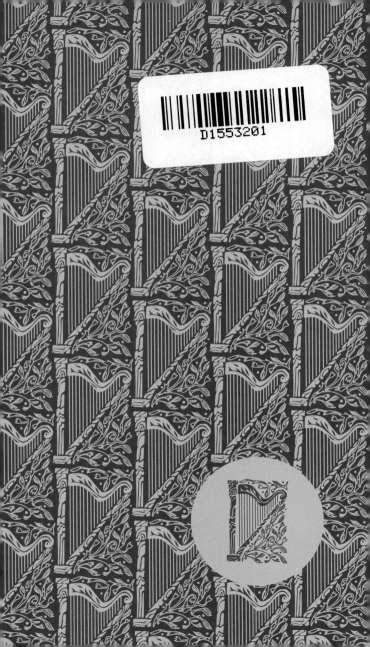

"Many churches today lack a theological vision of corporate worship, and in particular, of congregational singing. This book helps cast such a vision as a biblical, theological, and pastoral aid for us to sing with greater understanding—and gospel joy!"

—Matt Boswell,
pastor, The Trails Church

"Finally, a book on music in worship that is relevant and practical for any congregation! Magness illumines a spirituality of music with theological integrity while being generously ecumenical. I wish every pastor and church musician would read this book. You do not need a massive music program, ministry budget, or specialized staff to benefit from its counsel and apply the insight it presents with clarity and realistic suggestions. As a vocational church musician, I found it profoundly validating, encouraging, and reorienting."

—Miguel Ruiz,
director of parish music,
Messiah Lutheran Church
and Classical Academy, Keller, TX

"Worship for many is somewhat an auto-pilot experience. That doesn't disable the value and influence of the church's song. But richer depths and appreciation are available to those who probe beyond the comfortably familiar auto-pilot. This book wonderfully blends a principled approach to the church's song (valuing its heritage) with flexible creativity (expressing the heritage) in ways that will help any congregation to be faithful, authentic, and impactful in its worship life."

—Bryan Gerlach,
director, WELS Commission on Worship

"In this delightful monograph, master musician Phillip Magness starts with the basics. He gives us the theological joy of recognizing the church's music as a preeminent resource in the Lord's care of souls, and this because it is a vehicle for the Word of God itself. From that theological grounding, Magness proceeds to unpack in a plethora of practical insights (certainly applicable to nearly any Christian tradition) ways for every congregation to strengthen and grow in its feasting on the Lord's song. I cannot recommend the work highly enough to all who lead or plan worship."

—William Chancellor Weedon,
catechist at Lutheran Public Radio;
former director of worship for
Lutheran Church—Missouri Synod

"Cantor Magness is as serious as he is deft in translating the music of sacred ritual into language that is accessible without losing the Word—meaning the reverential dimension of what God does for us in worship. Too often, works like this either soar to parading rarefied theory or sink to becoming overly simplistic how-to manuals. This work does neither, yet is faithful theologically and useful for practice. All this, plus we gain authentic and current intercultural considerations for our lives of praise."

—John Arthur Nunes,
pastor, Pilgrim Lutheran Church,
Santa Monica, CA

"Every church musician is tempted to use superlatives when discussing the subjects of style and substance in worship music. In *Church Music: For the Care of Souls*, Phillip Magness measuredly and expertly invites us beyond our personal preferences to consider what we all can agree makes for the best music both in time and in eternity: the Lord's song given to us in his Word. Both wise and winsome, Magness is a worthy apologist and pedagogue, pulling from his many international and interdenominational experiences as a professional musician, cantor, and teacher to help us put into practice what Scripture makes clear regarding the Lord's song. This needed and necessary book will benefit all Christians making music in the church—those in the choir loft, pulpit, and pew."

—Katie Schuermann,
author and musician

"In this biblically-based, thoroughly-researched study, Phillip Magness draws upon Scripture and his personal experiences to pastorally and artfully craft an apologetic for the transcendent power of music—what he calls 'the Lord's song.' The church is desperately in need of rearticulating the wonder, the role, the purpose, and the power of music in her worship beyond pragmatism, and Magness helps his readers expand their vocabulary in expressing God's gift of music to his people."

—Joseph R. Crider,
dean and professor of church music and worship,
Southwestern Baptist Theological Seminary

Church Music

For the Care of Souls

LEXHAM MINISTRY GUIDES

Church Music

For the Care of Souls

PHILLIP MAGNESS

General Editor
Harold L. Senkbeil

LEXHAM PRESS

Church Music: For the Care of Souls
Lexham Ministry Guides, edited by Harold L. Senkbeil

Lexham Press, 1313 Commercial St., Bellingham, WA 98225
LexhamPress.com

Our books are available in print or as digital (Logos) editions in
Logos Bible Software.

Print ISBN 9781683597100
Digital ISBN 9781683597117
Library of Congress Control Number 2023930832

Lexham Editorial: Todd Hains, Elizabeth Vince, Cindy Huelat,
    Mandi Newell
Cover Design: Joshua Hunt
Typesetting: Abigail Stocker

23 24 25 26 27 28 29 / IN / 12 11 10 9 8 7 6 5 4 3 2

For Cheryl, my dear wife, who accompanies
choirs so beautifully, and for the faithful
musicians who volunteer their time
and talents each week to lead their
congregations in the Lord's song.

Contents

ACTS 20:28

Pay careful attention to yourselves and
to all the flock, in which the Holy Spirit
has made you overseers, to care
for the church of God,
which he obtained
with his own
blood.

Series Preface

WHAT'S OLD IS NEW AGAIN.

The church in ages past has focused her mission through every changing era on one unchanging, Spirit-given task: the care of souls in Jesus' name. Christian clergy in every generation have devoted themselves to bringing Christ's gifts of forgiveness, life, and salvation to people by first bringing them to faith and then keeping them in the faith all life long.

These people—these blood-bought souls—are cared for just as a doctor cares for bodies. The first step is carefully observing the symptoms of distress, then diagnosing the ailment behind these symptoms. Only after careful observation and informed diagnosis can a physician of souls proceed—treating not the symptoms, but the underlying disease.

Attention and intention are essential for quality pastoral care. Pastors first attentively listen with Christ's ears and then intentionally speak with Christ's mouth. Soul care is a ministry of the Word; it is rooted in the conviction that God's word is efficacious—it does what it says (Isa 55:10–11).

This careful, care-filled pastoral work is more art than science. It's the practical wisdom of theology, rooted in focused study of God's word and informed by the example of generations past. It's an aptitude more than a skillset, developed through years of ministry experience and ongoing conversation with colleagues.

The challenges of our turbulent era are driving conscientious evangelists and pastors to return to the soul care tradition to find effective tools for contemporary ministry. (I describe this in depth in my book *The Care of Souls: Cultivating a Pastor's Heart.*) It's this collegial conversation that each author in this series engages—speaking from their own knowledge and experience. We want to learn from each other's insights to enrich the soul care tradition. How can we best address contemporary challenges with the timeless treasures of the Word of God?

In the Lexham Ministry Guides you will meet new colleagues to enlarge and enrich your unique ministry to better serve the Savior's sheep and lambs with confidence. These men and women are in touch with people in different subcultures and settings, where they are daily engaged in learning the practical wisdom of the care of souls in real-life ministry settings just like yours. They will share their own personal insights and approaches to one of the myriad aspects of contemporary ministry.

Though their methods vary, they flow from one common conviction: all pastoral work is rooted in a pastoral *habitus*, or disposition. What every pastor does day after day is an expression of who the pastor is as a servant of Christ and a steward of God's mysteries (1 Cor 4:1).

Although the authors may come from theological traditions different than yours, you will find a wealth of strategies and tactics for practical ministry you can apply, informed by your own confession of the faith once delivered to the saints (Jude 1:3).

Our Lord doesn't call us to success, as if the results were up to us: "Neither he who plants nor he who waters is anything, but only God who gives the growth" (1 Cor 3:7). No, our Lord asks us to be faithful laborers in the service of souls he has purchased with his own blood (Acts 20:28).

Nor does our Lord expect us to have all the answers: "I will give you a mouth and wisdom" (Luke 21:15). Jesus, the eternal Word of the Father, is the Answer who gives us words when we need them to give to our neighbors when they need them. After all, Jesus sees deeper into our hearts than we do; he knows what we need. He is the Wisdom of God in every generation (1 Cor 1:24).

But wisdom takes time. The Lord our God creates, redeems, and sanctifies merely by his words. He could give us success and answers now, but he usually doesn't. We learn over time through challenges and frustrations—even Jesus grew over time (Luke 2:52). The Lexham Ministry Guides offer practical wisdom for the church.

MY PRAYER IS THAT YOU GROW IN HUMBLE appreciation of the rare honor and responsibility that Christ Jesus bestowed on you in the power and presence of his Spirit: "As the Father has sent me, even so I am sending you" (John 20:21).

Father in heaven, as in every generation you send forth laborers to do your work and equip them by your word, so we pray that in this our time you will continue to send forth your Spirit by that word. Equip your servants with everything good that they may do your will, working in them that which is well pleasing in your sight. Through Jesus Christ our Lord. Amen.

Harold L. Senkbeil, General Editor
September 14, 2020
Holy Cross Day

Prayer for the Ministry of Music

SINCE THE EARLIEST DAYS OF THE CHURCH, Christians have used holy Scripture to shape and inform their life of prayer. The structured prayer below invites pastors and laity to pray for the ministry of God's word in the midst of the congregation. It can be used by either individuals or groups—in which case a designated leader begins and the others speak the words in bold font.

In the name of the Father, Son, and Holy Spirit. Amen.

O LORD, open my lips,
and my mouth will declare your praise. Ps 51:15

He put a new song in my mouth,
a song of praise to our God.
Many will see and fear,
and put their trust in the LORD! Ps 40:3

We will tell the next generation the praiseworthy
deeds of the LORD,
his power, and the wonders
he has done. Ps 78:4

Glory be to the Father and to the Son
and to the Holy Spirit;
as it was in the beginning, is now,
and will be forever. Amen.

(Then a hymn or psalm may be sung)

Let us pray.

Lord, have mercy;
Christ, have mercy;
Lord, have mercy.

That God would bless those who sing his song
with love for those who sing with them, and
grant those who hear them a genuine desire
to hear God's voice;
That he would open the hearts of those who hear
to receive the blessings of the Spirit;
That those who lead the Lord's song would
be diligent in their duties, taking care to

maintain their skills and be ever mindful of
the Lord's intentions in their service;

Let us pray to the Lord.
Lord, have mercy.

That God would keep our voices in good health,
and lead us from temptations that would
harm or endanger them;
That he would preserve his song from all
who seek to silence it and guard us from
distraction;
That he would grant wisdom and discernment
to our congregations, that they may grow in
their understanding of worship, and joyfully
support the art of music in service of the
gospel;

Let us pray to the Lord.
Lord, have mercy.

Our Father who art in heaven,
Hallowed be thy name,
Thy kingdom come,
Thy will be done on earth as it is in heaven;

**And forgive us our trespasses as we forgive
those who trespass against us,
And lead us not into temptation,
But deliver us from evil.
For thine is the kingdom and the power and
the glory for ever and ever.
Amen.** *Matt 6:9–13*

Almighty God, grant that what we sing with our lips we may show forth in our lives and be shown forth in the lives of all who hear us. May your word dwell in us richly, resounding in our song, that we may be the people you intend; through Jesus Christ, your Son, our Lord, who lives and reigns with you and the Holy Spirit one God, now and forever.

Amen.

The Lord almighty direct our days and our deeds in his peace.

Amen.

CHAPTER 1

God Calls Us All to Sing

THIS IS NOT JUST A BOOK FOR MUSICIANS. I wish to address all who make decisions about congregational song: pastors, elders, worship committee members, and, yes, church musicians. The latter may be the ones who have developed the talents and skills needed for the church's "joyful sound," but musical knowledge alone is not sufficient for the task of singing faith into people's hearts. There is a special kind of art involved—an art in which each stakeholder is a participant. Like any art, it grows out of the practical knowledge that comes with repetition, habit, and awareness. It's apparent that the church musician does this, but whether one is an actual song leader or not, all who make decisions about church music practice this craftsmanship.

I contend that this craft, this business of singing—an activity that takes up significant chunks of time in the vast majority of Christian worship services—should be focused on the caring of souls through the art of music. All who are baptized have a stake in this and should know and cherish the church's song—the Lord's song, "The Song of Yahweh." So, while I address leaders throughout this book, the concepts I seek to advance here take root in the assembly, the actual chorus of faith. I hope, therefore, that readers will share what is learned here, so that congregations may understand and embrace what they are called to do every Sunday. The Lord gives all his people the gift of song so, ultimately, this is a book for all my fellow Christians.

The primary characteristic of Christian music is the sound of an assembly singing the praises of God. Even the most elaborate cantata or finely polished modern worship song grows out of this ethos: the eternal song revealed in Scripture, echoing through our hearts and voices. Every kind of Christian music seeks to capture this in some way, and there are many books about the history of church music and its various schools of performance. As Christians living in the twenty-first century, we have inherited a treasury of church music. In addition to that inheritance, we now have access to a rich variety of quality music sounded forth from different cultures all over the globe.

Yet at its core remain simple voices of faith, unaccompanied and unadorned yet eminently recognizable. Jesus taught that he knows his own and his own know him, just as sheep know the voice of their shepherd (John 10:27). The voice of the Good Shepherd now resounds throughout the world as the word is proclaimed in song, and we, the sheep, hear his voice echoing in the voices of our brothers and sisters.

Certainly, church music is more than just simple songs. The music of skilled musicians has great value when employed to proclaim the faith in more refined ways. But the ways in which we magnify the word should never predominate. Excellence in music has always carried the risk of becoming more about the music than the message—hence, the two millennia of debate over instruments, counterpoint, harmony, and even the qualities of melody. Wherever you or your congregation or denomination have landed in creating and maintaining boundaries in musical practice, my aim is to reorient you back to the source of all this: a holy God who gives a holy song to us. Whatever genres of music you may sing, at whatever skill level, this—the new song he has put into our mouth (Ps 40:3)—is what matters. So, let us consider how we make use of this gift God has given us so that we can develop the habits we need to support authentic gospel ministry through music in our congregations.

I realize this may sound presumptuous. The reader certainly may have grounds to ask, "How can you help me think about worship in my congregation when you don't know my people, aren't in my denomination, and likely don't play my style of music?" I believe I can, not because of any particular brilliance I have—though I think my breadth of experience does give my perspectives some value—but because God calls all of us, from every tribe and nation, to sing his song.

"The Song of Yahweh" is a significant scriptural theme. The new song he gives us puts a claim on us all—whether we are Protestant, Catholic, Pentecostal, Coptic, or Orthodox. The song transcends not just denominations but cultures and styles. It is a holy song, sung not as the world sings but as our faith sings. It was sung by Paul and Silas in jail and by Jesus and his disciples before they departed from the Last Supper toward the Mount of Olives. Singing breaks out among God's people from Genesis to Revelation and is a great gift for you wherever you may be on this earth in the twenty-first century. So whether your drums are timpani, a trap set, or a djembe; whether you rely on guitars, piano, or an organ; whether you have enough musicians to form a small orchestra or you use no instruments at all beyond the one God gave you, I believe I can inform and thereby help your worship considerations. Why? Because we are both singing the same song, regardless of the musical language in which we sing it.

Let me offer a personal story to illustrate how this book is more about content than method and how, because content drives and shapes method, the insights herein will be helpful for all who sing the Lord's song. I was honored once to serve as the clinician for a week-long church music camp for children in a town in the Deep South. The camp was organized by local music directors from four different traditions: Reformed, Methodist, Baptist, and Lutheran. Rehearsals were held at the different churches throughout the week, so I had an opportunity to discuss this business of singing with the various directors and pastors. While there was considerable variety of stylistic practices, from the guitar-led praise band of the Presbyterian church to a large pipe organ at the Lutheran church, there was a love for the art of music in each place and a desire for the children to sing the faith so that the word of God would dwell in them ever more richly.

I won't make any grand claims for my short time with them, but while the children were fairly tentative at the beginning of the week, they were singing robustly by week's end. And, while the ways in which each participating group sang the Lord's song were different, the sponsoring directors and their pastors agreed that the focus on "what we are singing and why" was helpful to them, even as the "how" was different in the ecumenical context and would be further different in their respective congregations.

I have seen the benefit of focusing more on the "what" than the "how" each time I have ventured professionally outside Lutheranism, whether I was the one being taught or I was teaching others. Similarly, no matter what your context is, the Lord's song in your midst will be continually improved and renewed when you focus on the song itself—its content, character, power, and many blessings—using the talent, faith, and skills the Lord has given you and your people.

Just as Moses and Miriam broke into song after they were delivered through the Red Sea, and Mary proclaimed her Magnificat in response to Gabriel's message, let us begin by considering that first love of our faith: singing the song of our salvation in Christ Jesus.

My life flows on in endless song;
above earth's lamentation,
I catch the sweet, though far-off hymn
that hails a new creation.

Refrain:

No storm can shake my inmost calm
while to that Rock I'm clinging.
Since Christ is Lord of heaven and earth,
how can I keep from singing?

Through all the tumult and the strife,
I hear that music ringing.
It finds an echo in my soul.
How can I keep from singing?

What though my joys and comforts die?
The Lord my Savior liveth.
What though the darkness gather round?
Songs in the night he giveth.

The peace of Christ makes fresh my heart,
a fountain ever springing!
All things are mine since I am his!
How can I keep from singing?[1]

CHAPTER 2

You Shall Have a Song

THE LORD GIVES US A SONG TO SING. Throughout the Scriptures, God's people are inspired to sing as they express their joy at God's saving acts. The Holy Spirit inspires the word of God, so these songs are also inspired. Also contained in holy writ is an entire hymnal—the book of Psalms—in which God's people are equipped to sing of their salvation, put their trust in God's promises, pour forth their laments, confess their sin, and rejoice in the steadfast love of the Lord.

These songs formed the corpus of worship in Old Testament times and were so closely identified with God's presence that they were often referred to as "the Lord's song." From the Song of Moses and Miriam (Exod 15:1–18, 21) to the Song of Habakkuk (Hab 3), the songs of prophets and psalmists by whom God spoke were considered to be the holy song of Israel. Isaiah identified the Lord himself with this holy singing, proclaiming, "The LORD GOD is my strength and my song, and he has become my salvation" (Isa 12:2), and the prophet Zephaniah proclaimed that the Lord who is in our midst sings himself (Zeph 3:14–20).

These songs were meant to be sung. They were not only described; they were commanded. In the Old Testament, there are thirty-eight prescriptions to God's people to sing. An entire tribe, the Levites, was set aside to perform priestly functions that included leading the people in song—most richly described at the dedication of the temple (2 Chr 5:12–14). There is little doubt as to what God wanted his people to sing about, as the Scriptures tell us what was sung. In singing the Lord's song, the Lord himself physically inhabits his people as lungs, larynx, and mouth are dynamically engaged and the whole body resonates with the word. In this way, the Lord inhabits the praises of his people (see Ps 22:3)—a presence just as real as when the ark of the covenant was brought into Solomon's temple and the divine glory filled the house of God.

The psalms also let us know that the Lord's song is given for our benefit, both individually and corporately. God doesn't need our song—we even anger him when we think our songs are some sort of meritorious sacrifice (Amos 5:23). While the Lord's song sung in faith certainly pleases him, just as a child's voice pleases her parents, it is really intended for our neighbors. Those who hear the Lord's song are strengthened (Ps 42:8) and comforted (Ps 77:6), and we ourselves are blessed as we sing (Ps 71). God's great goodness moves us to joyfully remember his mighty deeds "with all [our] might" (1 Chr 13:8). In psalms, hymns, and spiritual songs, we give thanks and are filled with joy (Isa 51:3).

To paraphrase our Lord in John 14:27, the song he gives is not the world's song, but his own, that as we sing it, our hearts would not be troubled and we might not be afraid.

The Lord's song also is a means by which the Holy Spirit carries the good news of salvation into all the world. Those who do not yet believe can be convicted by the Lord's song ("Many will see and fear and put their trust in the LORD," Ps 40:3). The Irish composer of modern hymns Keith Getty is fond of pointing out how the song of Christians is "a radical witness" to the world.[2] It is truly a unique witness. As comedian, writer, and banjo player Steve Martin sang on a recording he made with the Steep Canyon Rangers, "Atheists Don't Have No Songs." Martin's song had such appeal when it appeared in 2010 precisely because it is true: there is no tradition of Buddhist or Hindu congregational song. And while Muslims do have chanted prayers and melodious calls to prayer from the minarets, the assembled do not sing a corporate song of Allah.

From the beginning, however, the people of Yahweh have sung, and they will not be kept from singing. The Christian's faith will not keep silent; we sing of his salvation, and the astonishing richness and range of Christian music testifies to the creative character of God himself, in whom "we live and move and have our being" (Acts 17:28).

We sing to teach the next generation the story of God's love—and we nurture one another in that story as the word dwells in us richly through holy song. We get few explicit instructions in worship in the New Testament, yet twice Paul exhorts us to sing psalms, hymns, and spiritual songs (Col 3:16; Eph 5:19). The word dwelling in us richly through the art of music blesses and encourages us, attracts listeners, and gives convincing witness of God and his loving, mighty deeds. It creates meaningful memories for both singers and hearers as it uses relationships of sound to connect and interpret concepts and bind them into our memories.

It shouldn't surprise us that music has such power. After all, music was God's idea. The Lord reminded Job of this when he rebuked him from the whirlwind, saying, "Where were you when I laid the foundation of the earth? ... when the morning stars sang together and all the sons of God shouted for joy?" (Job 38:4–7). Music accompanied creation and will accompany the new creation (Rev 19).

I find it interesting that the Job passage cited above, as well as Psalm 19, talks about the measuring of creation. God asked Job, "Who determined its measurements?" (Job 38:5), and Psalm 19:4 talks of the measuring "line" going out through all the earth, pitching a tent for the sun as the heavens declare the glory of God. The idea of measurable relationships ordained by God in his physical creation brings to my mind the measurable acoustic relationships one finds in music. The ancient Greeks were profoundly aware of the mathematics of such relationships and so placed music alongside arithmetic, geometry, and astronomy in the curriculum.[3]

This may seem strange to us in our STEM era. Today, with rare exceptions, academia places music firmly in the arts and humanities, but the logic of the ancients' choice of placement is simple and profound. Karl Paulnack, director of the music division at Boston Conservatory, summarizes the placement well: "Astronomy was seen as the study of relationships between observable, permanent, external objects; music was seen as the study of relationships between invisible, internal, hidden objects."[4] Though many today just think music is a matter of taste, musicians themselves readily understand its objective qualities. Tuning, harmonic progressions, proportional phrasing, and the like are central to our craft—and explain why musicians appreciate quality in diverse genres of music. The art of music has unique power to fix the mind where God wants it: on what is true, honorable, just, pure, and lovely (Phil 4:8).

It is no real surprise, then, that the Scriptures contain a lot of music in them, commend the songs therein to God's people, and extol their singing. And, as is the way of the word, the Spirit bestows blessing to and through those who sing the Lord's song, and they in turn confirm his steadfast love and faithfulness in their lives. I don't know if I've met a fellow Christian who does not have some personal testimony that includes music. This blessing is probably why so many in our congregations have strong opinions about church music and are not hesitant to voice them. Such sentiments can be frustrating sometimes, especially when not spoken in love, but we have these feelings because we care. The church's song—the Lord's song—means so much to us that, by faith, we desire to share that song. It's an intrinsic part of Christian witness.

Let me share a couple of particularly powerful moments during which the Holy Spirit kindled blessing in my heart through holy song. The first was a personal awakening, the second a joyful realization of the power of music to bless others.

The personal awakening happened when I was thirteen years old. Though I had been baptized at a Greek Orthodox church as a child, I was not raised in the faith. After taking me to a Methodist Sunday school for a short time in elementary school, my parents stopped attending church. I did visit a couple of churches with friends as I got older, watched some religious television, and sometimes read the Bible my Baptist grandmother gave me, but I had little understanding of what my baptism meant.

When my family moved to Texas, however, some neighbors invited me to their Lutheran church. I primarily attended for the youth group, but since my neighbors picked me up each Sunday, I also went to worship. A few months into that school year, on the Sunday after Christmas, the congregation sang a classic Lutheran chorale, "Let All Together Praise Our God." It is a hymn that teaches about the great exchange, wherein Christ pays the price for the sins of all people while granting us the reward we do not deserve. While I have always loved music, I never realized the importance of hymns until this point, viewing them almost as filler material. But that morning my heart was filled with joy as I began to understand and take hold of the unsurpassable gift we have in Christ:

Within an earth-born form He hides
    His all-creating light;
To serve us all He humbly cloaks
    the splendor of His might.

He undertakes a great exchange, puts on
    our human frame,
And in return gives us His realm,
    His glory, and His name.

He is a servant, I a lord: how great a
    mystery!
How strong the tender Christ Child's
    love! No truer friend than He.[5]

Paul wrote, "I will sing with the spirit, but I will sing with the understanding also" (1 Cor 14:15 KJV). That Christmas morning, I began to sing like Paul. And the longer I am in this work of leading Christians in singing, the more I am convinced that *singing with understanding* is essential to truly ministering through music. Anything else—even if it be a professional-caliber band with an amazing soloist, a sublimely beautiful choral work, or an impressively-performed Bach cantata—is noise. It may be a most joyful noise, but it is not the joyous sound called forth by the Lord of heaven and earth.

Later, as a young professor teaching music at a community college, I began to understand how hymns deeply touched my fellow believers in a way that more closely bound us together as brothers and sisters in Christ. I knew that other believers had awakenings and epiphanies in worship similar to what I experienced as a teenager, but I had not yet perceived the power of the congregation's collective voice. Whether this was due to the musicianship in my high school congregation, my obtuseness, or the acoustics, I don't know.

What I do know is that my first Christmas at Hope Lutheran Church in Friendswood, Texas, gave me a foretaste of the feast to come, when all the saints in Christ will worship at the throne of the Lamb in his kingdom (Rev 5:11–13). This happened as the congregation sang, "Of the Father's Love Begotten."[6] The thirteenth-century plainsong used for the text helped me imagine the congregation's voice joining the concert of the cloud of witnesses cheering us on, but most impressive was the simple clarity and strength of the assembly chanting in unison, supported only by light organ accompaniment. I obtained a cassette recording of the service and, plopping it into an old, portable Panasonic tape player, listened to it for weeks as I drove around the Galveston Bay Area.

Thus began my journey from a rather secular young musician to one who found my calling as a church musician. Over the following three years I devoted more and more time to the music of my congregation and even served as the musician for a mission congregation twenty-five minutes away for two of those three years. I moved from supplementing my teaching income by playing jazz and pop piano gigs to doing more and more for the church—even starting a youth ensemble at my congregation. I joined professional church music associations, started attending conferences, and began to read voraciously on church musicianship topics. Finally, I decided to leave academia and pursue full-time service in the church. When asked for an explanation, I was fond of saying at the time, "I've realized that, when I'm in my fifties, I'd rather be improvising on 'Salvation unto Us Has Come' rather than 'I Want to Get You on a Slow Boat to China!'" Now that I'm almost sixty, I can attest that this was—and is—most certainly true.

The Lord's song is different from the songs of mortals. It is different because it has a unique story to tell: the great salvation the Lord delivers for you and for me, his people. The Lord gives a song that delivers the same message as the rites prescribed in the books of Moses. When our sons and daughters ask, "What does this mean?" one can answer in the same way Moses instructed, saying, "By a strong hand, the LORD brought us out of Egypt, from the house of slavery" (Exod 13:14).

"Egypt" for us comprises different enslavers— the devil, the world, and our sinful nature—but we were in bondage nonetheless and, in Christ, we have been set free. As Zechariah sings, "Free to worship him without fear, holy and righteous in his sight, all the days of our life."[7] We are the new Israel, and, beholding the fulfillment of salvation in Christ Jesus, our song is even greater, instructing not just one nation of their deliverance from sin and death but announcing this good news to all the world: "Oh, how abundant is your goodness, which you have stored up for those who fear you, and worked for those who take refuge in you, in the sight of the children of mankind!" (Ps 31:19).

This wonderful story of goodness is the song the Lord gives to his church.

CHAPTER 3

God's People Want to Sing

THE LORD DOESN'T JUST GIVE US A SONG. GOD gives us faith to sing it. Indeed, as we are filled with the Holy Spirit, we have greater motivation to sing than any other in the world. Though the devil, the world, and our sinful nature seek to silence this song, theirs is a losing battle whenever and wherever the people of God are freed to sing his praises. Don't be fooled: even people who say they can't sing or don't want to sing are moved to join in the eternal song when they are led with sensitivity to their souls.

Take, for example, a group that many music teachers might consider to be the toughest customers: junior high students. I have worked with all age groups over the past thirty years but have often found my greatest joy working with the hesitant, changing, and insecure voices of middle schoolers. Still a long way from adulthood and yet not really teens, they know they are no longer children and are often eager to grow up and move on—even as they cling to the security they still rightfully cherish as children. Their liminal age makes the choirs they sing in candidates for both painful failures and spectacular successes. In this way, they represent all of us sinner/saints: ashamed and even afraid of our voices yet eagerly desiring to join the chorus of God's joyful throng.

One year, working with a middle-school choir in the Chicago area, I broke off a smaller group of eighteen voices from my forty-voice parochial school choir and had them form a special ensemble that met once a week after school. They were a talented group of treble singers who did a nice job of singing three-part repertoire, both accompanied and a cappella. They were skilled enough that they had little trouble taking on René Clausen's "Psalm 100"—a piece usually sung by high school and college choirs. They were not typical of most Christian middle-school choirs.

One day, we had time to discuss what they understood—and how they felt—about choral music ministry. I asked them to write down the reasons they sang in choir, and the answers they gave were a great example of how readily people grasp the power of the Lord's song once they truly begin to participate in it. Their answers may not correlate directly to proof texts, but they clearly showed the students' appreciation for the gift of the Lord's song and an understanding of its purposes. They said they sang in choir to:

1. Raise spirits

2. Sustain culture

3. Bring people together

4. Sustain people on their journey

5. Have an impact on people's lives

I think these are pretty good goals for any church choir member to have. The raising of spirits evokes the sursum corda common in Western communion liturgies: "Lift up your hearts!" The desire to sustain culture shows how much these kids loved their church. They knew Christian culture is something special and that they had received an authentic tradition of worship in the music of our Lutheran family. Whether they sang a Reformation chorale, a Bach aria, a contemporary psalm setting, or a modern hymn, they knew they were part of a living heritage—and they loved it.

The goal of bringing people together might pertain to any choral organization, but in this context they were talking about something more than merely building community. The Christian choir doesn't build community for community's sake; it participates in the Spirit's work of calling, gathering, enlightening, and sanctifying the people of God as they magnify God's word in song. Through the word they proclaim, the choir becomes a tool of the Holy Spirit, as the church—the *ecclesia*, the "called-out ones"—is constructed through the ears that hear their holy song.

In their answer that music "sustains people on their journey," my students recognized that the word people sing at church stays with them throughout the week. Music makes lasting impressions on people's memories. Between the persuasion of melody and the power of repetition, the word of God often endures in the faithful's ears long after sermons are forgotten. From psalm antiphons to powerful refrains to impressive hymn stanzas to sensitive preludes or anthems, the singing we share together in worship brings lasting comfort and joy. Pastors and musicians who work closely together are able also to amplify the preaching each Sunday. This helps the people to gladly hear and learn God's word and thereby take hold of all the blessings that come to them as the Lord's gracious activity is revealed in the present and taken into their hearts.

These same spiritual tools work the same wonders regardless of age or demographic, for we share in the same Spirit (Eph 4:4–5). While it is true that the musical constructs should adapt accordingly, it is not our melodies or our harmonies or our rhythms that sustain faith but the word of God resounding in our hearts. Our faith hungers for it and so eagerly repeats the sounding joy as, per Isaac Watts's "Joy to the World,"[8] we prove the glories of God's righteousness and celebrate his truth, love, and grace.

I initially didn't care for my students' response that music should have an impact on people's lives. "Impact" is a word that can reflect a consumerist attitude on the part of the hearers. But those who sing the Lord's song deliver not the superficial impact of entertainment evangelism but the real impact that God delivers for all: the forgiveness of sins in Christ Jesus. The gospel makes all the difference in our lives, so we rejoice that we can use the gift of music to proclaim that same gospel, that those who hear our song may know the peace, hope, and cheer Christ freely gives from the cross.

This is what happens when we sing of Jesus, the Christ, whose word is our very song: the faithful are gathered, spirits are raised, our communion is nurtured, faith is increased, and lives are changed— all through the gospel power of this song the Lord has given us.

No wonder we want to sing!

CHAPTER 4

The Lord's Song

THE SONG OF CHRIST IS DIFFERENT FROM THE song of the world. It is different not because of a style but because of a substance: the Word of God, who has come into this world of death to bring us life. It is, therefore, truly an *alien* song.

As mentioned before, just as Jesus gives us peace "not as the world gives" (John 14:27), so he gives us a song not as the world sings. When Jesus told his disciples of the promised Holy Spirit, the Helper, he did not specifically mention singing. He did, though, point to his word and the keeping of it and assured the disciples that the Spirit would help them to "bring to … remembrance" all that he had said (John 14:26). The Spirit keeps us in the Word, and the Spirit and the Word are one with the Father. Thus, as our singing brings to remembrance the word of God, it is a Spirit-empowered and Spirit-enabled song. God gives us a song to sing and the faith with which to sing it.

Because of the word it conveys, the Lord's song is at odds with the world in every land and age. Perhaps most especially, it even opposes the people of God whenever and wherever we have forgotten him. From the beginning, when the commandments were given, the Lord has given song as a means to keep his word in remembrance. Those entrusted with the Lord's ministry are called to teach it, to "put it in their mouths, that this song may be a witness for me against the people of Israel" (Deut 31:19).

Whether recalling the stories of salvation, instructing in the law, or rejoicing in God's promises, the Song of Yahweh testifies of the One who is the Way, the Truth, and the Life. God's people may sing Scripture, a paraphrase of Scripture, or a song that faithfully recounts their experience of the Word and gives true testimony to that which is revealed in the word. In each case, the song is a gift from God that his people are called to take to heart: "For it is no empty word for you, but your very life, and by this word you shall live long in the land that you are going over the Jordan to possess" (Deut 32:47).

Because this song is a testimony against sin and the world's idols, it is not welcomed by those who oppose the Lord. The devil does not want us to hear it, let alone sing it, and the world seeks to silence, muffle, and distort it. We see these forces at work today in the cultural decline of lyricism, the societal shift away from homespun music toward listening to professional entertainment, and the movement in general music pedagogy away from skill development.

Yet the word endures, and we are called to sing it—even during pandemics. In doing so, in whatever time or season, we are blessed to "bring to … remembrance" (John 14:26) the great and merciful deeds of the Lord, as God inhabits the praises of his people (see Ps 22:3 KJV). This is not our doing, as if God is so happy that we've decided to praise him that he then deigns to come among us in some spiritual way. Rather, the Lord comes among us in the song he has given us to sing.

I began to perceive the distinction between generic religious music and the powerful holy Song of Yahweh when, as a young man, I directed a community children's chorus. By this time in my development as a church musician, I had come to understand that some Christian music was more spiritually nutritious than others and that certain musics[9] were, for various reasons, more effective in ministry. As I gained this understanding, I began to perceive the profound authenticity of the Lord's song as an aural tabernacle in which he dwells.

My ears were opened one summer when a Mennonite couple brought their three precious daughters to audition for the choir. I admit I did not have high expectations for them as, in response to a question about previous music education, they had written "homespun" (literally!) on their audition sheet. While I no longer remember what their audition piece was, I do remember the conviction with which they sang it. It was not the conviction of emotion but rather of reverence. They clearly understood what they were singing and who they were singing about, and they cared more about the song itself than being accepted into the choir. God wasn't with them because they were singing; they were singing because God was with them.

As you might imagine, I did accept them into the choir. A few months later, as I got to know the entire family better, they invited me and my wife to visit their church on a Sunday evening. It was an experience that, for me, drove home the desire of the faithful to sing the Lord's song and to sing it well, regardless of the styles and conventions of their particular tradition. The music was of a different tradition from mine, different instruments were used, and the architecture and some of the worship practices were not what I was used to. But the Song of Yahweh was heard for the edification of all as the Lord was present in the singing of psalms, hymns, and spiritual songs by those whom the Spirit had gathered that evening. This is something all too many Christians miss as they war over worship: the Lord's song does not rely on instrumentation, architecture, or any particular melodic tradition. The Lord's song is simply music that is initiated, governed, and driven by the word of God.

And because the Spirit sanctifies us through his word, we are sanctified as we sing, which makes us desire to sing and play well. History bears witness throughout the centuries to this, as the highest levels of artistic music enjoyed the world over rest on a foundation of God's word. While some traditions have only a cappella music in their services, the legacy of church music as a whole formed the basis of classical music and substantially shaped all forms of modern music, including the melodic and harmonic contexts of today's popular music genres—yes, even those opposed to the gospel! This really shouldn't surprise us, as the devil does not create but only perverts.

The extension of the influence of the church's music over instrumental as well as vocal music should also not surprise, as Psalm 150 calls all human instruments to be incorporated into the eternal song. So, as we sing and accompany our song with instruments, we are being driven by the Word of God, who comes into our hearts to dwell among us. The Spirit moves us to join the chorus of our fellow believers and embrace their ballad as our very own. We who have "put on Christ" (Gal 3:27) are in Christ and, finding our being in him, want to play and sing actively and skillfully (Ps 33:3). To be sure, "skillfully" does not imply a one-size-fits-all standard but rather the skill that comes from experience or *habitus*. When one loves what one does, one gets better and better at it. So has music flourished among Christians.

Playing skillfully brings in those objective elements of craft I mentioned earlier when referencing how the Greeks included music among the sciences. We have STEM today; they had AGMA: arithmetic, geometry, music, and astronomy. The art of performance incorporates the science and mathematics of music. Hearers may not know why some music sounds better than others, but even the musically illiterate can tell when things are out of tune or out of time. Sure, higher levels of music require higher levels of skillfully listening—and one needs to take care not to elevate the art of music beyond the listening abilities of the congregation as well as beyond their singing abilities. In one context, a hand drum and five-note scales may be all one has to work with and so will limit how quickly a congregation might grow beyond that. In another, one may have a Psalm 150 consort and a harmonic vocabulary that embraces the full chromatic scale—and a congregation attuned to appreciating the richness such a musical culture has to offer. Wherever we are between those points, we are called to use the best we have and play in tune with the gospel with music that suits our time and place.

Does this mean that style is unimportant, and that the only thing that matters is aesthetics? No, it is more nuanced than that. Mere fideism, no matter how sincere, won't do. In a 1954 radio address, President Dwight D. Eisenhower—who was baptized ten days after taking office in 1953 and under whose presidency the US Congress adopted the motto "In God We Trust" and added the words "under God" to the Pledge of Allegiance—said that faith was a defining characteristic of the American ethos. In a 1954 radio address, he said that Americans "by the millions ... speak prayers ... [and] sing hymns, and no matter what their words may be, their spirit is the same: in God is our trust." But the fideism so popular in his era, sometimes then summarized as "I don't care what a man believes so long as he's sincere about it!," is sorely misplaced. As much as we might rejoice in Eisenhower's embracing of the faith, he was wrong on a crucial point: *the words do matter*. Common sentiments may help bind a nation together, but they don't bring forth the kingdom of God. If the words don't confess Christ, the spirit is not merely different, it is opposed—no matter how sincerely they are believed or sung.

So it is with church music. One may make a joyful noise and delight many with virtuosic skill or appealing style. But neither is sufficient, no matter how sincere. What matters is getting the people to sing what God has given them, so that his promises, grace, mercy, and holiness may be called to remembrance and ascertained by those who participate in it. Thus, a special kind of musicianship is called for, one that springs from a *habitus* of singing the word and leading people in singing the Lord's song. This *habitus* nurtures the skills needed to sound the praises of God and summon the holy prayers of his people in whatever cultural context they may be.

Much of what I have so far said sounds a bit theoretical. I believe that as you read, many implications will be made clear. Nonetheless, some ambiguity will remain because the Lord's song transcends genres of music just as the word of God transcends all human societal bounds. To truly apprehend the Song of Yahweh, one must resist jumping to issues of musical style. Stylistic considerations are not unimportant, and they will be considered later, but it is important not to let labels get in the way of our understanding. The focus must first be on what God has for us to sing. If one wants to recognize the Lord's song, the key is to remember what God himself has to say about it. Only then do we begin to understand its height, depth, breadth, and width.

CHAPTER 5

Substance Over Style

My Mennonite students were clearly convicted not by how much they loved singing but by how they loved what they were singing. Their story illustrates not that we grasp the transcendence of the Lord's song by pursuing diversity but, rather, that we embrace a diverse set of musical genres because the Spirit has gone out into the world and made us one people out of every tribe and nation (Rev 5:9).

The cultivation of different styles simply for the sake of those styles themselves reinforces divisions among Christians and sends the wrong message to the world. One example is the practice of having multiple services in different formats to please various factions of the congregation, as it tells the world that our music preferences are more important to us than the Christ who unites us.

Instead, if we value singing the Lord's song over keeping the people satisfied with music they like to sing, we will discover and embrace songs from a range of generations and cultural backgrounds as long as they contribute to our life together in Christ. Rather than offering one service as a kind of museum for Christian nostalgia and another as an effort to catch up to the world or compete with some popular ministry, each congregation should take hold of the living heritage the Lord has set before it through his word and in his people. This heritage broadens as the various cultural backgrounds and even languages are incorporated, deepens as it encompasses a variety of styles in expression of the congregation's faith, and soars to new heights as it embraces the art of music in service of the gospel.

And it can do all this while maintaining the basic flow that characterizes Paul's admonition to do all things in good order (1 Cor 14:40). That order may look different in different places, just as a basic dance step such as a waltz can be executed in a variety of ways. But a waltz is not a waltz without a certain combination of steps, and worship flounders when it loses its proper focus. Above all, worship should lead us to comprehend the riches of Christ, which means the Lord's song in worship must echo the height, breadth, and depth of his love for us. Simply put, we should think about our singing just as our Scriptures speak about our Christ:

> For this reason I bow my knees before the Father, from whom every family in heaven and on earth is named, that according to the riches of his glory he may grant you to be strengthened with power through his Spirit in your inner being, so that Christ may dwell in your hearts through faith— that you, being rooted and grounded in love, may have strength to comprehend with all the saints what is the breadth and length and height and depth, and to know the love of Christ that surpasses knowledge, that you may be filled with all the fullness of God. (Eph 3:14–19)

This limitless love we sing extends into eternity. Luke's account of the transfiguration says that Moses and Elijah were interrupted in their conversation when they were taken from heaven back to earth to be an example for Peter, James, and John (see Luke 9:28–36). He says they were discussing Jesus' exodus (see Luke 9:30–31)—precisely the deliverance John heard the heavens singing about in Revelation. Once we start looking at worship from a biblical perspective ("What would Moses and Elijah want to sing?") rather than a human one ("What sounds are trending right now?"), we will be able to talk about style in a way that serves the Word rather than letting other factors drive our worship. When considering what Moses and Elijah would want to sing were they to drop in on our worship service, we choose songs that would echo the whole company of heaven as they sing the praises of the Lamb before his throne.

This truth is clearly seen when we look back at times in the church when style prevailed over substance. I recall being at a music conference where someone brought out some particularly bad examples from the 1920s. I have also seen my fellow church musicians chuckle at other well-intentioned efforts from much more recent decades that now seem impossibly passé. One example is the band SonSeed singing "Jesus Is My Friend" in a light new wave style. (Look it up if you'd like a smile.)

Another is some Anglicans' infatuation with the style of Frank Sinatra in the 1950s.

But my intention here is not to make fun of failed church music of the past. Rather, I bring this up to illustrate an even stronger point: even if the church can succeed in being "hip" for a moment, the world will immediately move hip somewhere else. Not that one can't bring back one of the exceptional hits from such efforts with some positive outcomes for the gospel—many times I've enjoyed singing an oldie-but-goodie from a 1970s Jesus Freak musical titled *Meet God, Man!*—it's just that the returns from such repertoires rapidly diminish. To quote the late Rev. Dr. Al Barry, former president of my own church body, the Lutheran Church—Missouri Synod, one role of the church is to hold fast to the "unchanging feast in a fast-changing world."[10]

The core problem with all of this is that music is, by its very nature, driven by a desired sound. It is not, at its core, word-driven. Indeed, the lyrics are often an afterthought. Whether it's the beat of the Charleston, the lush chords of the jazz era, the punky grooves of new age, or something else, when the point is the soundtrack, the proper focus is lost. The texts are commonly contrived to fit into the prescribed sound instead of driving that sound, and as long as the sentiments are religious and sincere, they are deemed acceptable. But the likelihood is that because the words have been subjugated to the soundtrack, they have been compromised. This is what happens when church music is only valued for its psychological effects, not for its ability to magnify the Word, teach the faith, and proclaim the story of God's love.

All of this is not to say that beats, rhythms, chords, and melodies are not valuable. They certainly are. A good text may find its ideal expression over a peppy beat ("Christ Has Arisen, Alleluia"),[11] benefit from some jazzy chords ("How Clear Is Our Vocation, Lord"),[12] or even embrace a hip groove ("Gabriel's Message" as sung by Sting, for example). But such music succeeds over time in the church—and is valued as good art even by secular musicians—because it is driven by the words, not by the beat or the harmony.

That song by SonSeed may make some chuckle today, with its anachronistic style, but it had the right message: Jesus is indeed our friend. The great good news is that he calls us friends, even though we are unworthy servants. But without the lyric

42

element—the word—music cannot proclaim that message. We love because God first loved us; we sing because the Lord himself is "[our] strength and [our] song, and he has become [our] salvation" (Isa 12:2).

Thus, above all else, the song of the church is driven by the word. Even if it be instrumental music that evokes the word in the hearers by means of association, the lyric element reigns supreme. Music driven by harmony, rhythm, or texture obscures or ignores the word and is, at most, mood music. It may be useful on occasion to soothe Saul, but it is not a sufficient vehicle for sounding forth the trumpet of salvation and proclaiming the triumph of our King.

CHAPTER 6

The Newness of God's Song

BECAUSE THE LORD'S SONG IS ROOTED OUTSIDE of us, in the very person of Christ, the incarnate Word of God, it is a holy thing and, as such, alien to this world. While the notes and sounds themselves are certainly not a sacrament, they accompany that which is sacred: the faith-creating and faith-bestowing word sent into our world from the eternal Triune God. Just as Jesus himself physically intervened in human history by being born fully human and dwelling among us, so does the word enter into every age as the Spirit imparts the blessings of his grace into human hearts from generation to generation.

In this way, by virtue of its alien nature, the Lord's song is new in every age. Just as the good news about Jesus has been proclaimed for two millennia and yet is still new, so are hymns and psalm settings and sacred anthems still new even as the music may be centuries old—and even as hearers may be intimately familiar with the "old, old story of Jesus and his love."[13] For the word of God is "living and active, sharper than any two-edged sword" (Heb 4:12) and continually accomplishes God's desires and purposes among us (Isa 55:11). The newness is therefore a quality, an eternal new song singing about the eternally new thing God has done for us in Christ Jesus. The old story is always new. The new song may indeed be sung to a new tune, but it is still new when it is sung to tunes of old.

Understanding this newness helps us have a better understanding of how the Lord's song manifests itself in various musical styles. While some musical genres carry profane associations that may make them unsuitable vehicles for God's new song, the newness of life in Christ Jesus transcends societal fashions and various cultural developments. The music itself is neutral. While human singing is essential, no genre is uniquely suitable or holy. Unless soiled by profane associations, all music is intrinsically capable of being sanctified by God's word.

Thus, while there is always room for new music, there is also no need for the church to embrace a new musical genre every generation. While every generation contributes to the rich legacy of church music we can enjoy for our great blessing, all new sounds are subject to the same standard as old ones: they are sacred only inasmuch as they are bound to the word of God. Regardless of age, the new song is the Lord's song, proclaiming the steadfast love of the One who makes all things new.

According to Revelation, we will worship God forever (Rev 22:3). While the last chapter specifically mentions only kneeling and adoring, abiding in the light of the Lord, the context of the previous chapters indicates that this adoring and abiding will be consistent with the singing revealed in the heavenly places. Why would those who "[keep] the words of the prophecy" (Rev 22:7) become silent? Or worship with our bodies but not our voices? No, the eternal worship of God entails an eternal song—one that we can only imagine, but one we will enjoy forever.

This good news was incomprehensible to me as a teenager. I was a young man in love with music, yet when I was told by my pastor that heaven was going to be like a worship service that never ends,

I thought, "How boring." I loved choir, but I could not imagine an eternal song. Later, though, I realized that the Scriptures don't speak of the new song from a temporal perspective but from a qualitative one. Transcending time, the Lord's song is an everlasting melody that the faithful will never want to stop singing. It doesn't get old, because God doesn't get old. In this way it is a mystery—a wonderful, marvelous mystery. It is fitting that we choose music that enables, encourages, and invites people to take hold of the mysteries of the gospel, that in our singing together Christ may dwell ever more richly in our hearts.

Those who have read Harold Senkbeil's *The Care of Souls: Cultivating a Pastor's Heart* will recognize this understanding of mystery. Senkbeil correctly ascertains that "mystery remains forever inaccessible to human scrutiny. Yet mystery revealed provides access to the inaccessible."[14] He goes on to describe the five decades of marriage with his dear wife, Jane, and how there is "no way I can completely plumb the depths of the mystery of our love and life. That's the very nature of mystery. There's always more to learn."[15]

So it is with the Lord's song: there is always more to sing, for there is no end to the breadth and length and height and depth of God's love for us in Christ Jesus (Eph 3:18).

The eternal newness of the Lord's song has profound implications for how we judge music itself. This truth was revealed to me at a church musicians' conference where I had the pleasure of listening to a presentation by Roman Catholic pastoral musician Michael Joncas. I was intrigued as he succinctly announced his convincing thesis: "All human musics stand under the Judgment." It's true: we dare not elevate any one form of church music to be "the holy sound."

It was frankly astonishing to hear this repudiation of earlier Roman Catholic dogma from a Catholic priest. Yes, the Roman communion significantly reformed its worship practice after the Vatican II Council, but Vatican I had elevated Gregorian chant as superior to all other forms of music, and I had thought it was still somehow first among equals.

Regardless of how Joncas resolves these tensions in the Roman tradition, he is right that even the most excellent, rich traditions can become an impediment to the newness of the gospel— occasions of idolatry, even—when particular forms that grow out of those traditions are thought to be more holy than other forms of music. This is a tricky point, as there *are* commonalities between all genres of Christian music, but the takeaway was trustworthy and true: the Lord's song is eternally new and is thus never contained within any particular tradition of sacred music.

This dynamic is consistent with the nature of Christ himself. Just as the human and divine are wed together in him as one acting person—what theologians call the hypostatic union—so does Jesus, the bridegroom, enter into a holy union with his bride, the church. In Christ, we become "partakers of the divine nature" (2 Pet 1:4) in fulfillment of God's promises to make us a holy people (Lev 20:26). Accordingly, just as he incorporates souls of all generations into his body, the church, so does he also sanctify the music of all generations so that all who share one Lord, one faith, and one baptism may sing with one heart and one voice.

This is done not by giving us a holy musical style—there is no such thing revealed in

Scripture—but by giving us holy words to sing. Thus, each generation here in God's creation makes music in the reflection of our Creator in new and various ways as God comes anew to us each day, even as Jesus Christ is "the same yesterday, and to day, and for ever" (Heb 13:8 KJV). In this way, the Lord's song is simply an unfolding of the mission of the Holy Trinity. Just as the stars sing the Lord's song at creation, the new creation sounds forth from our lips as Christ brings light and life through the living voice of the gospel.

So even if the music in your tradition is purely a cappella—whether chant or chorales or hymns—there is still an ongoing dynamic as God has his way with his people throughout time in a manner that keeps his song fresh. If the music of your people is not doing that—if the singing has somehow become stale or tired—the answer is to return to the word and muse on it anew. At the same time, be on guard against any cherished music becoming something other than intended or even becoming an idol. The people may love your band, organ playing, or choir, but if they are not bound by the word of God in what they do and how they do it, their singing and music-making risks becoming the noisy songs of human pride that the Lord pushes far away from him (see Amos 5:23).

Let's face it: we Christians are a handful. We can simultaneously embrace the familiar styles we have come to understand and love and grow tired of their sameness and repetition. How much of this is due to our fallen nature and how much is written into our flesh is beyond my comprehension.

But I do know our Lord intimately knows our human frailties, as he became one of us and so shared profoundly human musical experiences. It is no surprise, then, that God in his wisdom gave us words to sing but left the notes and rhythms to us, thus keeping his unchanging and eternal holy word primary. Meanwhile, the wings of song that carry the word to us pass away just as the individuals who preach, teach, and sing to us pass away.

Certainly, God *could* have done it differently, in which case we would perceive the holy song in a concrete way, as some sort of holy composition. But when Paul teaches that "no eye has seen, nor ear heard, nor the heart of man imagined, what God has prepared for those who love him" (1 Cor 2:9), he goes on to say that we who have received the Spirit of God freely understand those things that natural people do not get. For "we have the mind of Christ" (1 Cor 2:16). Here Paul is clearly referring to the spiritual truths of the gospel, not the music by which it is sung here on earth—even as we do know there is a glorious sound in heaven to which we will ultimately join our voices (Rev 14:2–3). This is why there are people who may love some Christian music and yet remain ignorant of its message, while there are also those who are converted through its hearing. (Many in Japan, for example, have come to saving faith after becoming fans of Bach's cantatas).

So, while music is powerful and even offers a foretaste of the eternal chorus before the throne of the Lamb, saving power lies not in the holy song but in the word that makes it holy. This could lead us to conclude that music doesn't matter, that any sound will do, and that this book is a waste of time. Far from it: just as there is much in creation that gets in the way of ministry, and just as some ways of teaching and proclaiming the word of God are more effective than others, so it is with music.

Music can be an obstacle to the Spirit's work of creating and sustaining faith, just as mumbled preaching, insensitive prayers, disorganized teaching, and the like are impediments to the gospel.

Similarly, just as the Lord's work is accomplished through well-crafted sermons delivered with attentiveness to the hearers, prayers that illuminate both our need and God's loving disposition toward us, and Bible studies that faithfully teach God's truth in dynamic ways, so does he use excellence in music to sing faith into people's hearts. God has entrusted his ministry to us, and he calls us to be faithful. Here is where our creative energies lie.

CHAPTER 7

Finding the Right Mix

Yᴇᴛ ʜᴏᴡ ᴅᴏ ᴡᴇ ɢᴏ ᴀʙᴏᴜᴛ sɪɴɢɪɴɢ ᴛʜɪs ɴᴇᴡ
song so that its freshness is continually revealed
and God's word can dwell in us ever more richly?
The key to answering this question in any given
congregation is twofold. First, understand the natural fatigue that sets in when any music becomes
too familiar. Second, intentionally nurture enough
music so that the hearers move from being entertained to having a core set of quality songs they
will cherish just as they cherish the one who iden-
tifies himself with his song.

Discovering how best to sing the Lord's song
yields different playlists in different congregations, contexts, and traditions. To be sure, there
is a natural, healthy, and desirable overlap, which
is larger among congregations that share the same

confessions, traditions, or cultural contexts, but the best answer is unique to each community. Gene Edward Veith offers a helpful paradigm to consider in making these decisions. In discussing culture, Veith proposes the categories of pop, folk, and art.[16] He applies these categories generally to various aspects of culture, from food to literature, and I find it helpful to consider worship and music according to his paradigm.

As Veith defines it, popular music is music that is readily understood and enjoyed—even as it requires a high level of musicianship to execute. Moreover, the quickness with which it is embraced means it is also quickly loathed—hence, the reason pop music goes up and down the charts so rapidly and the songs that stay at the top of the charts for a long time eventually disappear for a long time.

For example, it is only now in the 2020s that we are beginning to hear Bobby McFerrin's "Don't Worry, Be Happy" again, whereas back in the 1980s it was one of the hugest hits of all time. The first a cappella piece to reach number one on the Billboard chart, it gained ubiquitous play on rock, R&B/hip-hop, country, and adult contemporary stations. The following year, it won three Grammy awards: Song of the Year, Record of the Year, and Best Male

Vocal Performance. Then it was practically gone. Since that time, it has been used in some films and probably did get some radio play, but almost twenty-five years went by before I heard it again. This is but one example. George Gershwin's "Swanee" is another. It had a longer run due to there being much less mass communication during its time, but then it became a bit of a comic reference before being set aside for decades.

The precipitous rise and fall of most popular music illustrates a pitfall of using popular music as the foundation for worship. I say this not to suggest that popular music styles have no place in worship. I think they are effective when one wants the assembly to quickly grab hold of something. But they don't have staying power. In my context, where we often sing refrains to contextualize psalms, I find popular styles to be very helpful in getting the people to sing those refrains right away. This works especially well because months, even years, go by before the same psalm verse will be used for such a refrain. There is no worry that people will get tired of it, and the catchiness of these refrains helps the Scripture verse stay with people throughout the week. But such refrains are not going to form a lasting repertoire, and they would make for a rather shallow collection of songs were they to be so enduring. So it is not a question of whether to make use of popular, readily accessible styles but rather how, when, and where to do so.

On the other side of the spectrum from popular music is art music. Like popular music, it requires a higher level of musicianship. However, unlike popular music, it is not so readily appreciated. This is because it is not designed to entertain as much as to stimulate. Thus, it requires attentive listening, which is greatly aided by beauty of performance—calling for an even higher level of musicianship. Indeed, art music only succeeds in worship when it is beautifully performed. It needs the attraction of that high level of performance in order to sustain attention. Yet, even then, it risks being just a diversion or distraction if the hearers are not directed and helped toward listening to it. Minds may wander or, as is all too common, people will use the opportunity to read the bulletin, go to the restroom, or visit with each other. Meanwhile, the choir that has no business trying to sing Handel will subject the assembly to what the congregation magnanimously accept as their friends' sacrifice of a joyful noise.

Again, don't get me wrong: just as there is a place for popular musical styles, I think there is a place for classical sacred music and new music written in classical or neo-classical artistic styles. I lead choirs in singing Schütz, Bach, Mendelssohn, Brahms, Berger, Schalk, Manz, and more. But in order to be something that truly ministers to people, not something that is merely tolerated, art music needs to be properly programmed and done well. To make sense and contribute to the proclamation of the gospel and the calling of all to faith, it requires a context where the assembly is disposed to give ear to it. When all of these things are in place, it is an extremely powerful vehicle for the living voice of the gospel. Where congregations have talented persons willing to dedicate their time to such excellence, it should be encouraged and embraced by the congregation. But, like a delicious sauce or an exquisite dessert, it is not the standard for the people's song.

That standard is best served by folk music, which can be found in the middle of the spectrum between popular music and art music. To be clear, I am not referring to a genre of music, with a specific style and instrumentation, for which someone like Joan Baez or Bob Dylan is known. Instead,

I am referring to a living tradition of song that can be sung by amateurs ("amateur" here simply means untrained or non-professional and should not be taken as an insult). Folk music, by definition, is music that is specific to a given community and that serves to bind that community together around a shared set of stories and traditions. Folk songs are meant to be sung by the members of the community, and as a result, they make use of simple and accessible musical constructs.

By contrast, both pop and art music call for some level of expertise and rehearsal in order for them to be executed well. As a result, they typically leave the people primarily in the role of hearers. That doesn't mean the people can't play a role in worship when pop or art music is used, but they do not play the primary role. As the Lutheran composer Carl Schalk reminded me, the congregation called to sing the Lord's song in the Lord's house on the Lord's day is made up of "non-musicians, coming without rehearsal." They need songs that allow them to fulfill this calling successfully, not songs that are beyond their ability to sing.

This is why the limited range, simple rhythms, clear accompaniments, enduring traditions, and strong melodies of folk music provide the best means for today's Levites to lead all the tribes of the new Israel in the Lord's song. For most of us, that folk music lies in our denominational hymnals. It also includes new music composed with the people's voices in mind, such as that written by Keith and Kristyn Getty, Stephen R. Johnson, Matt Merker, Sandra McCracken, and Marty Haugen, among many others. Such tunes may not be as catchy as pop music, but that is why they have greater staying power. And while they often form the basis of excellent art music, from Bach cantatas to Aaron David Miller organ fantasias, they are accessible, enduring tunes intended for all to sing. Nurture a core set of them, and your congregation will sing sturdy hymns throughout the year with the same gusto with which they sing Christmas carols.

This does not mean that music that leans firmly into the realms of popular or artistic music has no place in worship. Each has its place. Though this book is a call for the church to reclaim the people's song, I want to caution against overreacting to our society's marginalization of communal music in favor of arts and entertainment. There is real testimonial value in the expressive capabilities of such music, particularly as it gives voices opportunities to proclaim great things in a way that attracts people to enter into that experience. A performance of a Broadway classic like "Still Hurting" by a voice like Amy Bloom's or Ariana Grande's delivers the feels and enables listeners to sympathize with something they otherwise might not share. It can inform understanding of others and encourage us in Christ to better love our neighbor. Both art and pop music have been excellently used to connect congregations with the experiences and feelings of biblical characters, moving congregations deeper into the story and edifying the body of Christ.

But we must take care in this. Music is powerful. Like all powerful tools, it can be misused. While there is cathartic value in appropriating the sentiments of an artist's performance, faith is not born of sentimentalism, nor does the cultivation of sentiment increase our faith. One does not fear, love, and trust in God above all things on the basis of one's feelings but through the work of the Holy Spirit. His burning in our hearts comes as we encounter Jesus, which does include meeting him in the testimony of faithful witnesses in song but does not include artistic manipulations that may also stir our hearts. Whether found in the cultivated aesthetics of high church music or the emotive impact of a popular artist, spiritual confusion results when art's goal is to move people rather than bring people to Jesus and bring Jesus to them.

Thus, the more that music is rooted in the common song of the people, even as it should be attractively and even artistically performed, the closer it is to the assembly's voice and more suitable for providing a musical context for uniting God with his people. While certainly music in the folk spectrum can also feed sentimentalism (particularly through nostalgia), its lesser focus on the performer, the transparency of its musical constructs, and the direct engagement of the assembly in its production all serve to promote the message of the music rather than the sounds of the music. Simply put, music centered in the folk range of the spectrum places the heart of the Lord's song in the hearts of God's people.

Also, while the care of souls can include growing in the understanding of the story through vicarious testimonies, art and pop music both rely on the intermediary of the performer, and so the listener will always have the sense of sharing *someone else's* experience. Sure, people can take such ballads as their own—just as teens often do with their favorite rock anthems—but the music that brings people into owning the faith has the character of folk song, whether sung together or enjoyed through singing to one another. With both pop and art music, the medium carries the message of someone else's faith, missing the *pro nobis* ("for us") that is intrinsic to the Lord's song.

Because we are one in Christ, ours is a shared experience. Musical styles and genres that call for all to participate therefore reflect and manifest the profound truth that we each inherit all the blessings of Christ and may consider them our own. In Christ, we are always part of the story. Therefore, we always have a share in the song.

CHAPTER 8

The Lord's Song (Con)Textualizes Us— In Every Context

We need to take a turn here. It's tempting to take these truths we've covered—that God gives us a song to sing, a song that comes from himself and is always new—and boast as Peter did before he fully got the gospel, telling the Lord what we'll do for him. Yes, the sacrifices of thanksgiving and praise remain, even as the sacrifice for our sin has been fully paid, and so "it is good to sing praises to our God; for it is pleasant, and a song of praise is fitting" (Ps 147:1).

But the Lord did not leave us orphaned. He sent us the Spirit, who leads us to sing with understanding (1 Cor 14:15). We sing not because God is on his throne every Sunday morning looking at his proverbial watch and waiting for his children to do a song routine for him but because he has given us a song for our blessing. Yes, he delights in the singing of his children, but it is his good pleasure to do more with our singing than just receive it.

Whether he was writing to the Corinthians, the Ephesians, or the Colossians, Paul makes clear that we ourselves are blessed when we bless the Lord with our psalms, hymns, and spiritual songs. God uses our thankful hearts to have his way with us as we sing. Singing the song the gospel has initiated in our hearts—a song fueled by the word and driven by the Spirit—we literally sing faith into each other's hearts. We are formed in faith as music helps us know the word by heart, as it shapes our prayers, and as it teaches us. It literally "textualizes" us.

This is a key point at the heart of what it means to have the word of God dwelling in us richly through the art of music. God's word is performative. It does what it says, accomplishing in us his sanctifying work (John 17:6–8; 2 Tim 3:16–17). Indeed, the Psalter—the Bible's hymnal—begins with this theme and returns to it consistently. Psalm 119, the longest psalm, is solely devoted to this idea, via an acrostic in which each letter of the Hebrew alphabet begins a set of eight verses that explain and extol living by the just decrees of the Lord.

This stands in stark contrast to the postmodern view of texts. Today the world considers texts malleable and debates the utilitarian value of their deconstruction. God's text is different; it is holy. His thoughts are not our thoughts (Isa 55:8), and his mind and ways are infinitely higher than ours (Rom 11:33–34). The higher a view one has of Scripture, the higher one should esteem the Lord's song.

The genres of music that are used vary in different contexts, so there is some contextualization that takes place for music to be employed most effectively, but the ultimate contextualization is not our work, but God's. The word of God is "living and active" (Heb 4:12) and accomplishes God's intentions. The Holy Spirit thus literally textualizes each one of us as we sing the story of his love (Ps 89:1); it forms us according to the word of God we sing. Though our song is shaped by culture, the Lord's song is ultimately countercultural. It is a super-genre above all genres of music, manifesting the people of God in each time and place, from generation to generation.

This makes sense because the ministry is not our own but the Lord's. While it is easier to see some things clearly directed toward people as the work of the Lord—whether it be the sacraments, preaching, or even our works of mercy and love toward our neighbor—music ministry can sometimes seem to be more our own work. Yet it, too, is the Lord's. As he works through the ministries entrusted to us—both pastoral and auxiliary—God is at work. As he establishes the work of our hands upon us, his church, our song mystically takes on his character as we put on Christ. In different ways, in the various genres of music throughout the world, a commonality develops by which the sound of his voice is increasingly recognized even as radically different people sing it among the diverse cultures of our world. Each style in which it is manifest is transformed, creating an atmosphere that draws worshipers to lift up their hearts.

There really is a difference. Even with the more entertainment-driven models of Contemporary Christian Music (CCM) that seek to sound like various popular music genres, one can quickly tell in a new city which stations are playing the Christian forms. The difference is more profound in worship music, regardless of continent, moving from more entertaining sounds to more meditative ones, from technical virtuosity and tonal novelty to lyricism and beauty. Perhaps musicians pick up this a little more quickly than others, but many a fellow believer has reported the same thing.

One day, in my work as a sacred music educator in francophone Africa, I was in a taxi in Pointe-Noire, Congo, when I had an experience that once again drove this point home. The radio was on, and I realized I was hearing something different from what I had heard before. While I have always readily recognized when I hear various Christian musical imports from France or Westernized forms of African music sung with French texts, this song was being sung in Lingala, an African tribal language I do not understand. But the quality of the singing, the use of harmony, and the sense of reverence that prevailed made me think this was not a typical pop music text, even though it was not manifesting Western influence—that is, the adaptation of some Western instruments and modern studio equipment—any more than the Afropop I normally heard.

So I asked the taximan if the music was Christian. I was informed that, yes, this was a song about Jesus and his love for us. As a result of this encounter, I discovered a brother in Christ (who happily came back to pick me up from my hotel on subsequent mornings) and was reminded of how the Lord's will is done in all things—including the art of music.

Yet while the one holy song has its way of making itself known throughout the world, we must not forget that there is no one type of music— no holy sound—uniquely worthy for the church to use. Our fallen nature inherently discredits our music; "all human musics stand under the Judgment."[17] This insight is important not just for what it says about approaching all musical styles with humility but also for what it says about our own preferences. We are wise to be humble about them—and to lead our people into the same humility. No matter how much we may like a particular style or piece of music or how strongly a member may feel a certain song is *the* thing the church needs to be singing, we do well to remember that the gospel is ultimately not about the soundtrack but about Christ's saving work on the cross for all people. More on that in the next chapter.

CHAPTER 9

There Is No Holy Sound

PEOPLE HAVE STRONG, MEANINGFUL ASSOCIA-
tions with the music that accompanies their youth,
conversion experiences, and other significant life
events. In ministry, one needs to recognize and
affirm this reality for the sake of ministering to
others, but it is also important to recognize this
disposition in ourselves and to lead the people in
our care to recognize it for the sake of living in
community.

This doesn't mean that you, as the music leader,
can't sing something you love or introduce that
song a member has on her heart, but you must
think critically about it first. What would you be
singing instead if your, his, or her favorite under
consideration didn't exist? Is the new piece truly
better for the occasion? Consider all who will sing

and hear the piece in question, and honor them as your brothers and sisters—not as guinea pigs for liturgical experiments.

At the same time, teach your people to open their ears and their hearts to fresh expressions of the Lord's song—or, conversely, to sing oldies. This is increasingly necessary in our global, multicultural age, as each one of us is called to sing faith into the heart of the person in the pew in front of us—a person who likely has a differing favorite or preference from ours. God is glorified more when we sing what our neighbor needs to hear than when we sing what we may happen to want at the moment.

Let's face it: the temptation to view our own favorites as best for ministry is strong. Certainly, there is much to be said for that which we love. Indeed, such love is essential for ministry because one can't really deliver something one doesn't possess. But often this means learning to love something we didn't love before. I will discuss that at more length later. For now, as we focus on how the Lord uses music to form and empower his people in every context in which the church may be, let me keep the focus on the issue of style preferences themselves. They have such potential to divide and, unfortunately, they often do.

It's an easy trap to fall into. We associate certain soundtracks with dynamic, faith-building, and faith-sustaining experiences we have had, so naturally we want to share them with others. As mentioned earlier, there is nothing wrong with favorites, and they are even a good thing in and of themselves. But the mind works by association, and while the gospel associated with our soundtracks is very much worth sharing, the music by which the Lord worked to indwell his message deeply into our hearts may not resonate as well in the hearts of our neighbors.

This is especially true in the early stages of a community's growth in sharing together the music they love—a process that requires trust in the leadership and in one another so that all can accept there is no agenda at hand other than the gospel. I'll add here that big, essential steps forward are made when pastors, cantors, choir members, elders, influential families, and all the usual suspects accept that some personal favorites won't be found worthy or appropriate for the whole community for either musical or doctrinal reasons.

The elevation of personal preferences into a holy sound perceived to be uniquely suitable for authentic worship is at the root of most of our worship wars. I had a chance to delve into this issue rather deeply while preparing for a keynote address to my church body's national worship conference back in 2008, as I took time during a sabbatical to visit a dozen congregations in three states.

These visits included attending worship, interviewing pastors, and having focused conversations with congregants. I had intentionally sought out congregations that were known to tout excellence in worship while offering both *traditional* and *contemporary* services. A few of the larger congregations even offered an additional *blended* service. My main goal was to learn what their different worship formats held in common, so that I could see what they considered essential and what they considered optional and to see how the various assemblies sang psalms. Along the way, however, I gained a profound observation, which I included in a keynote address I gave at the Institute on Liturgy, Preaching, and Church Music in 2008 and have shared often since then:

The "contemporary" service in a typical LCMS [Lutheran Church—Missouri Synod] congregation is a service that features, almost exclusively, a single style of music promoted by a segment of the congregation at odds with the previous practice, and the "traditional" service in the same congregation is whatever the congregation was doing at the time the new service was started. Both services have remained, since the division, essentially the same, as the natural process of a congregation working together to make worship decisions was replaced by having services characterized by musical preferences. Moreover, those musical decisions were intrinsically conservative, as the "traditional" group viewed anything "new" as belonging to the "contemporary" service, and the "contemporary" service was committed to a branding characterized by the single musical style embraced when that service was started. Thus, both services became frozen in time.

While sometimes a new service was initiated for other reasons, in most cases—and

in dozens of cases I've come across in subsequent years—the origin of having different
worship times according to different worship
"styles" grew chiefly out of music preferences.
Such considerations of "soundtrack" characterized the new services whether they were
driven by pastoral preferences, a desire to
attract different people, or by internal congregational squabbles. People who claim they
"just can't worship" with this or that kind of
music convinced congregations, de facto, to
confess by their actions that the music that
divided them was more important than the
Christ who unites them.

This is not to say that one group didn't
have a better idea as to what music would
be best, but in each case some people were
allowed to be wrong, and the community
as a whole failed to "bear each other's burdens and so fulfill the law of Christ" (Gal
6:2). While short-term peace may have
occurred, in the long run such division frus-
trates the spiritual growth of the congregation. Limited by their personal musical
preferences, worshipers are more turned

in on themselves, and thereby become less aware of the whole church.[18]

The assertion of some mystical holy sound is particularly pernicious because it largely comes from those who love music—that is, the very people who lead music in our churches and/or make decisions about it. Those less inclined to care about music are often just happy that some compromise or provision has been made so that there can be more peace in the congregation—even as they might not like the decisions so much themselves. It is wise to talk to the non-music-oriented members about the issue, as they often have more wisdom about music in churches than one might expect. They may not be musicians, but they sing the music the church sets before them each week— or at least they are expected to. One should listen to what they have to say. Listening does not mean agreeing, but it does entail learning, and you may find that what you learn persuades you.

Such conversations have greatly helped me in my ministry. For instance, when I was a young cantor in Peoria in the 1990s, I inherited the congregation's attempt at contemporary worship. They had decided to have this service on Saturday nights, as they didn't want the different format to chase away folks from the two Sunday morning services.

When I arrived, I saw a small group of twenty to thirty worshipers doing Vineyard music, camp songs, and old gospel hymns, led by a guitarist and song leader who played tambourine. Setting aside issues I had with the order and content of the service and focusing just on the music, I started seeking out the individuals who came each Saturday night to talk to them about the service.

I learned that most of them chose to attend for reasons other than the music: work schedules, health reasons, preferences for smaller groups, and the like. When I asked them about the music, they were charitably hesitant to be critical. They mentioned liking a couple of the songs but expressed a desire for more hymns from our Lutheran hymnal. They wanted to sing more familiar songs as well as music that was more in accord with our doctrine. They liked the more relaxed and homespun format and didn't necessarily want an organ-led service, but they definitely wanted something most would call more traditional.

So we made the order of service more like Sunday's, kept the guitar and occasional hand percussion, added piano (and, eventually, a bass player), and brought Lutheran hymns back into the service. We also started singing psalms at each service, with accessible refrains for the assembly, and chose a small number of contemporary songs we thought would work well. These were supplemental hymns that were singable for the congregation, accorded with our doctrine, and fit the ensemble well musically.

Over the ensuing five years, the service grew from twenty to thirty people to around one hundred people each Saturday night, in a congregation that also grew on Sunday mornings. The growth happened for two reasons: one, because more people overall were coming to the church; and two, because everyone felt that the Saturday night service was not a different church but *their congregation, too.*

Let me make clear that, even as we who lead worship seek to make good decisions and do things in the proper order, it is God who calls, gathers, enlightens, and sanctifies the church, contextualizing us in every place. I have only described how his work was done in one place. But worship leaders are the ones whom he calls to participate in his creative work, so, for the sake of the ministry entrusted to us, let's keep considering best practices while giving to God all the glory.

In light of that charge, let me add a third, powerful reason I believe the congregation in Peoria experienced the growth it did. The unity we enjoyed in having a contemporary service that was comfortable for the majority of the members made members much more likely to invite their friends and neighbors. It isn't good outreach to tell people, "Come to my church, but only at a certain time when they are worshiping the way I think they should." In Peoria, no longer did we emphasize something that divided us. We kept the focus on Christ, who is truly attractive. And we grew.

This leads to a final, key observation about this canard of a holy song that some argue we should have. As I mentioned, such ideas are usually significantly driven by my fellow music folk. The strong preferences many musicians have for either classical or pop music not only impacts ideas about which songs to sing and how they should be accompanied, it also gets in the way of the people singing on a practical level. It's not just that the movement away from the folk part of the spectrum leaves out the people; it also leaves them behind musically by taking away vocal models that invite them to participate in the singing. Both pop and classical music are intended for listening. It's the folk music in the middle that is more participatory.

Both classical and pop music are harder for non-singers to sing; more importantly, the actual singing in those styles does not invite people to sing along. Indeed, while talented singers can be a great blessing for a congregation, the chief vocal model should be a voice they can relate to. The people in the pew may by impressed by the impassioned soul singer or moved by the artistry of an operatic voice—and both can play a constructive role—but such voices say, "Listen to me." The people need to be led by voices that say, "Sing with me"—that is, voices they can naturally match.

As proof of this, consider the national anthem. When it is led successfully, the leader does not use an operatic vibrato, nor does he or she add the improvisatory melismata of the soul singer. Instead, a natural, healthy voice sings the melody straight, in a singable key. The leader's job is to summon and lead a common song, not offer a virtuosic or emotive performance.

If we want our people to sing so that they can be more fully textualized by the Lord's song, we must remember who they are. I'll say it again: today's congregations mostly consist of non-professionals, coming without rehearsal. Sing things they can sing, and lead them in ways that make them feel they can join in. As they join the chorus of faith, their hearts will be changed for good.

CHAPTER 10

Fides Quae, Fides Qua

HEARTS CHANGED BY THE GOSPEL REALLY DO have something to boast about. That's why there is such unique joy and vigor in communal Christian singing. The world boasts in its works, but she who has Christ boasts in her Lord. Jesus exchanged his life for ours that we might truly live! His story has become our story, and that is why we lift our hearts and voices. We sing of who our God is, of what he has done for us, of what he continues to do even now in our own lives, and of his trustworthy promises to be fulfilled in the coming age. Whether we are singing of past blessings or future promises, our devotion finds expression in objective and subjective forms: we sing of the faith by which we are saved, and we sing of our experience of that faith.

The ecclesiastical terms for these two categories are *fides quae creditur*, the "faith that is believed," and *fides qua creditur*, the "faith by which it is believed." Here we have a valuable distinction between the objective faith we confess—however imperfectly we may hold to it or understand it—and our subjective experience of saving faith. The *fides quae*, which may be understood as "objective faith," thus embodies the content of Christian praise, as our song proclaims the story of God's love, who God is, and what he reveals to us in his word. The *fides qua*, the trust in God we experience through the gift of faith, forms the content of our adoration, as our hearts express our thankful love for all that he has done and continues to do for us. The psalms and the best Christian hymns draw on both the objective quality and subjective experience of our faith. Music and worship ministers should lead their congregations to realize and take hold of the fullness of the faith in which they participate by the power of the Holy Spirit. Embracing the fullness of grace upon grace, they help the faithful own the objective truths of God so that they may bask in the ever-increasing, evermore-joyful experience of faith.

Simply put, the *fides quae creditur* tells what life in Christ is; the *fides qua creditur* describes our personal grasp of these truths and our personal trust in them. Both the content (*quae*) and the trust (*qua*) are universal in different cultures and peoples. But the subjective dimension of personal faith leads inevitably to personal experiences of living out the word of God. And so we sing of both: the objective content and our various personal experiences. Personal experiences may include subjective testimony. Subjective testimony by itself may make fellow believers glad and even make some non-believers desirous of faith, but without the objective proclamation—so precisely described in the Latin theological term—faith is not increased. "Faith comes from hearing, and hearing through the word of Christ" (Rom 10:17). So while we do want to offer our hearts' adoration, we need to remember that responses to the singing of subjective experiences depend upon the relationship of the hearer to the singer and to the hearer's own feelings relative to the ones being described. Responses to singing the works of the Lord—the received proclamation of objective faith, the faith that is believed and confessed—however, rely on the Holy Spirit.

The former is an encounter with a fellow human; the latter is an encounter with God. This is not to say we shouldn't sing about our share in the story. How can we not? We cannot take ourselves out of the equation. God uses our voices. We just need to make sure that in the process we are giving voice to Jesus, so that when people hear us they can hear our Lord. They need to hear about God's love toward us much more than our love toward him.

Consider the anecdote I shared about the personal encounter I had as a young teen when I was awakened by the gospel while singing, "Let All Together Praise Our God." The hymn simply, yet profoundly, describes the great exchange, even using those very words. While I had understood at an abstract level that Jesus died for my sins, it was upon hearing the words of the hymn that I moved from a juvenile agreement to a set of Christian truth propositions—Jesus is Lord, God is Triune, sin is bad, and Jesus died because of it—to comprehending how Jesus' life and death actually delivered *for me* forgiveness, life, and salvation. I had heard people talk about their *experience of salvation* for years—at Boy Scouts, visiting churches, and youth group—and certainly the pastor at this church had preached Christ as well. But the *procla-mation of the faith that is believed, the objective truth of the gospel,* put *into my ear and onto my lips in song,* is what finally moved me from various religious thoughts and notions all rooted in the law to actually taking hold of the grace and mercy prepared for me in Christ Jesus.

While salvation does not depend on either my feelings or the depth of my understanding, that day in my youth I fell in love with Jesus—and that is a good and glorious thing. I was already a baptized child of God, yet through this hymn the Holy Spirit kindled faith into flame. Grasping his love in a way I had not before, how could I not rejoice and give thanks for one who took on my sins and gave up his life for me—a God who gives me "his glory and his name"? I quoted part of the hymn earlier; here's the rest of it, so that you can see how the hymn tells the story and then applies it to you and me:

Let all together praise our God before
     his glorious throne;
Today he opens heav'n again
     to give us his own Son,
     to give us his own Son.

The Father sends him from his throne to be
    an infant small;
And lie here, poorly manger'd now
    in this cold dismal stall,
    in this cold dismal stall.

Within an earthborn form he hides
    his all-creating light;
To serve us all he humbly cloaks
    the splendor of his might,
    the splendor of his might.

He undertakes a great exchange, puts on
    our human frame;
And in return gives us his realm,
    his glory and his name,
    his glory and his name.

He is the key and he the door to blessèd
    paradise;
The angel bars the way no more!
    To God our praises rise,
    to God our praises rise.

Your grace and lowliness revealed,
    Lord Jesus we adore;
And praise to God the Father yield
    and Spirit evermore.
    We praise you evermore.[19]

So we do not remove ourselves from the story. We who sing the praises are the ones who have been given God's glory and name, after all! As another favorite Lutheran hymn sings, we proclaim, "What great things God has done for me!"[20] But without the good confession of how God is the chief actor in this story, our song lacks the "one thing needful" and, in the process, robs our testimony of its power. If we are to sing Israel's song, then the song must be the story of God's love (Ps 89), even as it includes our own experience. As saints have shown throughout the ages, we are called to decrease as Christ increases.

Similarly, as we grow in faith, our story conforms more and more to the word of God. Our song should reflect this—and our singing should help us attain ever more fully all that God the Father has prepared for us in Christ Jesus. Simply put, it is proper, right, and salutary for us to tell the story in song and for us to love to sing it—but rather than hymns such as "I Love to Tell the Story," which simply extol our telling of that story, we need hymns that actually do tell the story.

When our testimony does this, it has impact. The living and active word moves people to recognize the authority with which we sing. Our personal experiences may or may not be perceived as authentic, but there is nothing but truth in the word of God.

And this impact does bring testimony of our personal experience of faith, such as in the many comments and letters I have received over the years from people who have been awakened and enlivened in faith through the proclamation of my choirs. One visitor came pretty close to this theological outline, noting in beautifully simple words that she loved how "the singing had life to it" as she could sense how "they were thanking God as they were singing about Christ." You see, though she likely knew nothing of the distinction between *fides quae* and *fides qua,* she had picked up on how faith takes hold of God's song and makes it one's own.

Too often church choir members consider their service only to be their personal sacrifice of praise. At best, they then see their sacrifice as an offering on behalf of the assembly. I call that "vertical worship": it's just them and Jesus, and we get to watch.

By God's grace, though, I have been blessed to work with choirs and soloists ready to move beyond themselves and let their voices be more fully devoted to ministry. The crucial difference lies in the understanding that our song should be not merely a personal sacrifice of praise but a participation in the proclamation of the gospel. One of my choirs even chose the name Proclaim so that people might better understand their participation in the ministry. Another chose the name Psallite to illustrate our emphasis on singing God's word.

This union of proclaiming both the work of the Lord and our experience of it is thus *horizontal*—from us to each other—as well as *vertical*—between God and us. The paradigm is beautifully cruciform: God empowers the singing, and we sing back to him and to one another, sharing the gifts he has given.

This cruciform image of the horizontal and the vertical in worship should call for more than just a balance in content—a consideration of the weighty beam of our personal experience supported by the heft of our confession of the faith, if you will. It also serves to remind us of the source of the faith, hope, and love of which we sing: Jesus Christ, crucified for us for the forgiveness of our sins, the outpouring of new life, and our eternal salvation from our enemies.

I like to illustrate this by drawing the cross with directional arrows, with the source of our song starting at the top (God-to-us) and then flowing out to others in testimony and back to him as a sacrifice of thanksgiving. When both the content and direction are aligned accordingly, the Christian congregation experiences the fullness of God's praise—complete with all the blessings that come from the word dwelling among us richly.

This picture of the Christian faith doesn't happen when the source, God, is not there. Merely implying or inserting God won't do either. Even as many may be moved by a powerful musical testimony exhorting them to do good works or telling everyone how much they love God, such music is really no more convincing than Dr. Phil or Oprah because it lacks spiritual power.

Without the testimony of Christ, the Holy Spirit will not accomplish the divine intentions God has stored up for us in his word. Sure, the Holy Spirit can do anything he wills, but God has established an order by which he deigns to be recognized and through which he has promised to work. Jesus said, "The words that I have spoken to you are spirit and life" (John 6:63). We are wise to take our Lord at his word rather than put him to some test.

Yet in our well-intentioned zeal to engage the lost, motivate the faithful, and be relevant to the world, that's what we do all too often: put our Lord to the test as we push boundaries, acting like little children. Take, for example, Christmas Eve about twelve years ago, when the Christian gospel group Avalon had a smash hit re-recording of Celine Dion's secular holiday song "Don't Save It All for Christmas Day." The song trended on the CCM charts and was performed in many a contemporary worship service across the land.

While one can—and many did—try to justify its use in worship by saying it was just an "exhortation to good works, like we get from Peter and Paul," the blessed apostles did not decouple such exhortations from the cross but grounded them in the new life we have in Christ. Just as a good sermon follows in the pattern of the scriptural witness we have of Christ-centered preaching, so should the song of the church be characterized by Christ-centered singing. Such lyrics as these would not have been sung by Paul and Silas in jail:

> Don't get so busy that you miss
> > Giving just a little kiss
> > To the ones you love.

Don't even wait a little while
    To give them just a little smile.
    A little is enough.
See how many people are crying.
    Some people are dying.

So don't save it all for Christmas Day.
    Find a way to give a little love every day.
Find a way 'cause holidays have come
    and gone
    But love lives on if you give on love.[21]

The rest of the lyrics are the same: life-coaching tips of the kind one gets on daytime network TV or in the magazines in the grocery checkout lane: no gospel, just an exhortation to be nice. "Love lives on *if* …" The words say nothing about how love lives because of Christ and what he did and does for us. They provide no reminder of the one by and in whom we love because he first loved us (1 John 4:19). There is no mention of the death and resurrection of Jesus *for us.* Love instead is going to "live" because of our works—this, in congregations that inherited the Reformation! Lord, have mercy.

Love doesn't live on because we are nice or do nice things. Love lives on because, through Christ, God gives us the Holy Spirit, who alone sanctifies us and kindles in us the fire of everlasting love.

And so we see the importance not just of balancing the subjective and the objective but of making sure that any subjective testimony we have and any good we wish to encourage must rest on the God of our salvation, who alone does good things (Rom 3:9–20) and from whom comes every good and perfect gift (Jas 1:17).

This bears continual repeating because it is so tempting for the purposes of pleasing congregation members to let them have what they want—whether it is something someone wants to sing or something they want to hear. But the care of souls is like the care of children. Just as we delight in satisfying our children and yet are careful in what we give them (Luke 11:11–12), we should also, in the care of souls, provide for the godly desires of their hearts (Ps 37:4) and not simply satisfy the demands of itching ears. Sometimes the most loving thing to do is to just say no.

The reference to Psalm 37 above helps us understand how this looks not just in terms of the quality of texts we choose but also the style of how we sing them. There is a character that is nurtured in music when one takes to heart Psalm 37:4: "Delight yourself in the LORD." This character is outward and upward focused, looking with one eye on God and one eye on neighbor. The performance of human-centered lyrics, on the other hand, nurtures a more inwardly focused style.

The year that "Don't Save It All for Christmas" came out, I heard from a relative who did not, at the time, understand the pitfall of focusing on a personal expression of faith rather than on the rich content of the faith. The congregation she attended was more focused on building community than on discovering the community that has already been created for us in Christ Jesus. She described what happened when a singer at her church sang the Dion song:

> There's a girl in the band who usually sings backup, but they gave her this solo on Christmas Eve. The usual lead singer wasn't there, and so she was sort of getting her chance. Well, we all just couldn't believe how she nailed this long note toward the end of the song. It was just amazing. And as she held it, we all just started to applaud. It was so awesome.

There are many who want to ignore the prevalence of such attitudes about worship in Christendom today and let everyone do what they think is right in their own eyes in the name of freedom. Certainly, our Lord gives us much freedom in how we are to worship him. But doing whatever pleases our ears is not what he has in mind for us. G. K. Chesterton observed that "the nineteenth century decided to have no religious authority. The twentieth century seems disposed to have *any* religious authority."[22] Along the way, we've seen many congregations move from freeing themselves from various denominational authorities to submitting themselves to the authority of the CCLI Top 100 list.

These are hard words, I know. So let me be clear and say that many congregations that have what is generally called "contemporary worship" have more discernment than this. Indeed, some have much more.

Still, the above story illustrates what permeates the repertoire that forms the song list of entertainment evangelism. It is a well from which many drink. I encounter stories like this every time I am on the road and visit a church's contemporary worship service. To be fair, I have encountered similar—just less emotive—sentiments, texts, and showmanship at liberal mainline churches that use a classical sacred music soundtrack to achieve the same human-centered, works-oriented, community-building goals. But regardless of the source or style of the singer-driven music, it is important to be honest about it.

Such examples illustrate the core issues we all need to keep in front of us, lest the slippery slopes of our personal style preferences lead us into consumerism or elitism. The above story was not intended as another backhanded swipe at contemporary worship or another volley in the worship wars. Indeed, I can offer other examples I have experienced where the praise band was more focused on singing the word of God and proclaiming the story of his love than the traditional service at another congregation.

I'll end this section of the book with one more example. Remember that singing school in Alabama I mentioned? One of the participating congregations was a Presbyterian Church in America (PCA) church. When I went to the church, I was at first disappointed that the pew racks were empty. There were no hymnals, just screens. I remembered previously meeting a couple from another Reformed tradition—the Christian Reformed Church—and being excited to discuss their denomination's *Psalter Hymnal* with them, only to be disappointed to hear, "We have that but don't use it. Our band covers CCM." So, beholding the stage, guitars, and drum set at the Presbyterian church, I confess that I thought I had run into something similar.

Upon meeting the PCA worship director, however, I discovered the church was singing psalm paraphrases and cross-focused hymns, not radio music, and emphasizing congregational participation. They were committed to singing the Lord's song, so content drove their method. The experience reminded me of the danger of imposing my preconceptions on a situation with which I was not completely familiar.

As I emphasized earlier, there is certainly room for *fides qua creditor* expressions in hymnody. I happen to think that a certain amount of it is essential. Great hymn writers like Paul Gerhardt (German, 1607–1676) have superbly incorporated the subjective experience alongside the objective truth extolled and confessed in our hymnody. Such hymns and songs continue to be written today. Faith moves us to sing, and it is salutary to extol one's heartfelt adoration of our Lord.

But the music of *my personal experience* alone can't sing faith into other people's hearts because it doesn't sing the story of God's love and proclaim his faithfulness (Ps 89:1). So its use for corporate worship is especially limited because it doesn't allow us to address one another and build each other up as Ephesians 5:19 and Colossians 3:16 instruct us to do with our music.

To help people understand this, I have found it wise to get people accustomed to hearing and talking about *the* faith instead of always saying *my* faith. This is similar to how it is helpful in regard to a church's life together for people to understand the work not as "*my* ministry" or "*your* ministry" or even "*our* ministry," but as "*the Lord's* ministry." It's not wrong to refer personally to one's faith, and it is good and salutary at times to sing a simple song of praise. There is certainly a place for Psalm 150 expressions in the life of the church. But we have a whole psalter of faith to sing about, and the riches of God's grace far surpass our own personal experiences of it, however inspiring they may be.

Ironically, those who promote the *subjective, experiential* repertoire of contemporary worship often claim that such music is necessary in the Divine Service for the sake of outreach. Yet there is often very little that is overtly Christian in these subjective songs of praise. How, then, can it truly be evangelical?

I'll say it again: listening to someone sing about their great love for God can certainly make an impression, but, at the end of the day, the impression is going to be about the singer. The truly evangelical music is the song that sings not of the singer's faith but rather the music that sings *the* faith. Only through the proclamation of the Christian faith, the objective faith that is believed and confessed, can music magnify the word and thereby sing faith into people's hearts.

CHAPTER 11

Discovering One's Voice

GOD BE PRAISED FOR GIVING US OUR VOICES! He has equipped us with a built-in instrument. But how shall we sing this song our Lord has given us? Tragically, common wisdom teaches that only a few can sing. Indeed, many churches today foster this view and, as a result, are filled with non-singers who are accustomed to letting the amplified sound of song leaders do the singing for them. The result is very little actual congregational singing and an illusion of worship in place of the real thing.

This is particularly ironic in the evangelical churches of the Reformation, who replaced the medieval choirs of clerics with vibrant congregational song. Now, in many places, they have replaced congregational song with a different group that, in effect, worships on their behalf. A primary task, then, for using the art of music for the care of souls is simply to get the people singing again. Fortunately, people really do love to sing (God made them to do so, after all), and there are winsome ways to help them find their voice.

In a culture that doesn't sing together much anymore, one may have to start from scratch, particularly with your new-member classes, but also at church potlucks and the like. Sing "Happy Birthday" (add a second verse that sings "God's blessings to you") at every opportunity. Add the common doxology to the end of congregational voters' meetings. And have fun! Take a moment out of Bible study and see how many groups can successfully keep a simple round like "Row, Row, Row Your Boat" going.

That's right: for this purpose, the songs need not be religious. Just get them singing again. Musing well—"good musing" as opposed to "good music"—is childlike. And the folk may only know a few songs from their childhoods. It may feel childish to start there, but it is not. It is tapping into a first love and getting a key into people's hearts. Simple refrains from hymns or choruses from praise songs can pick it up from there as you rebuild a singing culture in your congregation.

Make every effort you can. Back in the 1990s, the congregation I served had a vacancy in the youth minister position, and I was given a significant number of interim duties for a year. Knowing that many youth activities were outdoors, and wanting to lead them in singing in a fun and engaging way, I dove into practicing an accordion I had previously been given. As a keyboard player, I had always admired the portability of guitars, and this gave me the incentive to have a portable instrument myself. While I certainly could have led the singing outdoors with my voice and a hand drum, the accordion opened up more possibilities.

Over the coming year, the kids and I had a great time. And the surprise of the new youth minister was quite remarkable when he came to his first outdoor youth event and heard thirty-five teens robustly singing a through-composed[23] version of Psalm 141 ("Let My Prayer Rise Before You as Incense") from one of our liturgies[24] while I accompanied them on the accordion as part of our devotion. The lesson I hope you take from this example is to be creative and take advantage of all the avenues the Lord may open up for you to get people singing.

Meanwhile, there is a little trick that can vastly help liturgical congregations during the service. If your worship is participatory and your congregation is of a size where you need mics, *turn off the mic* when it is the congregation's turn to confess their sins, confess the Creed, say the Lord's Prayer, or speak some other congregational part. It is arguably the easiest way to help a congregation find its voice, yet so many places don't do this. Yes, at first they may stumble, but when they realize it's up to them to vocalize their part and that no one else is going to do it for them, they can and will step up.

For pastors who don't have someone at the soundboard to turn their mic off and on—though I would think someone can and should be found to do this—the alternative is for the pastor not to say those parts, just as the pastor should not say liturgical responses like "Thanks be to God," "Praise to you, O Christ," or other responses.

And pastors: regardless of whether the mic is on or off, I recommend that if you are in the habit of saying the congregational parts, you stop doing so. Again, there will likely be an awkward pause when you first make this change, and you should explain to the folks why you are doing it. But in the long run you will be teaching your people to *take ownership of their parts in the liturgy.* Let them have their "Amen"!

As your congregation begins to find its voice, you can make use of people, including yourself, who are willing and able to be vocal models for the congregation. If there is a new hymn, or just a somewhat familiar song, you are going to use in a service, line it out ahead of time.[25] In some traditions, it will be fine to do this right before you sing the whole song together; in others, this is best done a couple of minutes before the service begins, or when the offering is received.

At first, lining out can take a little more time. The congregation needs permission to fail, to be accepted, and to grow accustomed to the practice. The key to this is for the leader *not to sing along* when it is the people's turn to sing back. When they fail or need to try a line again, stay positive, say something like "Nearly right!," and model again. This is imperative not only so the people can find their collective voice and accept their responsibility to sing the Lord's song but also because *the only way the leader can evaluate whether to go on to the next line or to divide it up into smaller pieces is for the leader to listen to them.* If this process takes too long at first, take heart: you will have learned a valuable lesson about your congregation's real abilities. You can start picking simpler and more familiar songs with greater frequency, being careful that the next song you line out is an easier one.

This time of lining out can be extended for great benefit. While some traditions highly value quiet time before worship and others emphasize social time, almost all can make time for a period of "singspiration" before the service. In a more conservative, liturgical tradition, this might just be done on special occasions, with advance notice, such as, "Come early Christmas morning and choose your favorite carols to sing." (This is a handy way to head off complaints about someone's favorite carol not being in the service, by the way.) Consider also the hymn-sing tradition, such as Lessons & Carols in Advent on a Sunday evening, or an extended time of congregational song sometime during a week in Lent.

In other places, it can be a regular feature, perhaps once a month or during a time of renewal. It might even replace the sermon or complement a short homily on certain special occasions or unusual Sundays, such as when Sunday falls on

December 26. Such song-focused opportunities can be quite enjoyable and, in addition to encouraging people to sing, can reveal what the congregation's favorites really are and sometimes even uncover a hidden gem. It may have taken me another decade or more to discover "O Rejoice, Ye Christians, Loudly" had a parishioner not summoned it one Sunday morning in Peoria back in 1997.

As you learn what hymns your people love, you will learn what they have taken to heart. Though it is overused in some circles, there is much truth to the axiom attributed to Prosper of Aquitaine: *lex orendi, lex credendi* ("[According to] the rule of praying, [so is] the measure of believing"). Such was the wisdom of Ambrose of Milan, who instituted the singing of orthodox hymns for the comfort and strengthening of souls against the Arian heresy.[26] The craft of the care of souls through the art of music therefore involves discerning the people's song and then patiently and lovingly affirming that which is salutary while gently guiding the sheep into greener, more fruitful pastures of song.

This is no simple, mathematical task. Simply replacing one set of songs with another, purer set won't do. Instead, it is an art similar to the practice of medicine. Just as a physician needs to listen attentively to ascertain the dynamics of body and mind in the whole person, so does the music or worship minister need to listen to the people to ascertain the dynamics of their singing and their faith. *Lex orendi, lex credendi* is not a one-way street. Faith changes one's song just as one's song changes faith. So one needs to learn intimately both the congregation and the congregation's voice in order to nurture them into singing more richly of Christ and growing more deeply rooted in him.

This process can—and probably will—involve some hard knocks. When I was a young college professor, I was asked to take over directing the parish choir at the small church my wife and I were attending in Friendswood, Texas. I had wonderful memories of singing sacred music in high school and college choirs and had long wanted to sing some of that great repertoire in the context of worship. My wife and I had been singing with the choir for a while, but I had not found the previous director's choices to be inspiring. Here was my chance! I would choose classic chorale repertoire and set about inaugurating a new era of choral music for the parish.

My plan was a flop. It turned out I wasn't the solution. Instead, as always, the Lord was. As much as I wanted to introduce my new church choir to the great choral repertoire, they weren't ready for it, and they became frustrated.

This became clear to me one Sunday when, with limited rehearsal time, I had chosen a rather simple anthem with an accessible refrain and a suggestion in the score to have the congregation join on the refrain. The anthem had a piano rather than organ accompaniment. My choir liked the piece and learned it readily, singing it with freedom that Sunday morning and, with the readily agreeable refrain, getting their heads out of the score.

As they found their voice and got away from the notation on the page, something remarkable happened: they began to sing faith into people's hearts. The score called for the final refrain to be repeated. Inspired by the singing, I leaned over the edge of the balcony to better soak in the robust sound ascending from the nave. Then I spontaneously motioned for the pianist, my wife, Cheryl, to stop accompanying, and I directed the choir to keep singing. It was a moment I will always remember, as the congregation sang with the basses and altos while the sopranos and tenors carried a countermelody. I could tell the congregation loved it, too. Important lessons were learned as real ministry took place: the congregation is the primary choir, and the choir is called to lead them. The director trains the choir, summons the song, and prepares the repertoire, but the ministry is to the whole congregation. The director must therefore not only help the choir to sing better but help the congregation to find its voice as well.

This is not to say that singing some more challenging repertoire is excluded. There is certainly great value, for both choir and congregation, in proven sacred choral music sung beautifully. Such music transcends social boundaries and inspires both singers and hearers. It develops your choir, according to the ability of the singers, and expands the musical palate of the assembly.

But first people need to find their voice. I give thanks to God for providing an early lesson in that truth one Sunday morning, over thirty years ago, in that small Texas town.

CHAPTER 12

The Importance
of Listening

In the last chapter, I emphasized the importance, for the pastor or worship leader, of being quiet and listening when it is the congregation's or the choir's turn. That doesn't only apply to the church service. Listening to the people involves listening to them at all times, including when they share their opinions and complaints.

You probably don't need me to tell you that people have strong opinions about worship and are not hesitant to share them. The positive side of this is that it demonstrates that people care. The negative side is that it is not easy to be the target of criticism. I have learned two strategies for handling criticism that are immediately helpful when dealing with individuals. I have also found them to be helpful in advancing the conversation in some additional beneficial ways.

First, be thankful. When someone comes to you with a complaint or criticism, remember the alternative: to not come to you and to gossip or grumble instead.

So stop what you're doing and listen. Believe it or not, you may very well have something valuable to learn. Avoid being defensive and, instead, ask clarifying questions. It is vital when discussing worship to *be specific*. Find out what is really bothering someone. Often there is a larger problem that has nothing to do with you, the music, or the service. With patient listening and honest, open questions, you may well discern that there are personal conflicts and spiritual issues involved. You won't be able to solve those, and you shouldn't try, but your very listening is healing, particularly as the conversation moves you to pray for and with the person.

Second, inasmuch as you can, take note of the surface concern and take measures to address that symptom. It is rare in life and even rarer in church arguments about worship that you will explain your position with the result that your listener says, "You are right. I'm wrong. Thank you for convincing me with your brilliant defense of the thing you were doing that bothered me."

So don't try to win the argument. That doesn't mean you shouldn't explain your own thinking about the issue at hand. But just as you know you can't solve all their personal problems, admit to yourself that you can't solve their way of thinking either, no matter how much more you may know. If you listen, build trust, and establish a relationship with them, you can and will influence them. They need someone who will hear them, which is why they came to you. If you truly hear, they will appreciate your time and your ear. While they won't necessarily change their mind (and even if they do, they might not immediately admit it), you may discover in time that you have had an influence. Care more about the person, and the rest will come.

Here's an example. One Sunday afternoon when I was still a young church worker, I had just gotten home from church when I received a phone call from a distraught parishioner who had many complaints about the worship service. My wife had prepared lunch, but as the phone call dragged on, I told the family to eat without me. This dear sister had a load on her mind, and I needed to listen. Initially, the gripes were about hymns, the choir, and certain things she didn't understand about the services and how they were being conducted, but I sensed there was more.

As the conversation continued, a subtext of deeper concerns was revealed, most of which had nothing to do with me. She was bothered by things that had happened long before I arrived at the congregation, was still hurting, and needed to feel like she was still a valued member of the congregation. Taking care not to encourage harmful or destructive comments, I nonetheless acknowledged this parishioner's feelings and sympathized where I could with the various life experiences she shared. I rejoiced at her fond memories of her previous church and took to heart things she said about how there were "great things in the music library" the choir was no longer singing.

Upon sharing this conversation with the pastors at our next staff meeting, I learned more about this woman's strong opinions but also about some trials in her life and her steadfastness in faith. During our conversation, I had taken note of several of her complaints, ideas, and suggestions, and, a few weeks later, acted on one of them.

She had mentioned how sad she was when she saw that the "new" hymnal (introduced over a decade earlier, in 1982) had not included one of her favorites: "Come, Ye Disconsolate."[27] So, for our Lenten services that year—services she always attended—I brought that hymn back.

It wasn't my intention, but that small, simple act gained me a vocal ally and friend for the rest of the time I spent at that congregation. After I gave this dear woman one beloved hymn—incidentally, a very good hymn—it seemed I could do no wrong in her eyes. She was fine with all sorts of things after that and consistently complimented the choir and the hymns, even though I never used another hymn she had wanted or stopped doing a couple of the things she had complained about. Years later, I met my successor at this congregation at a conference, and he mentioned getting an earful from this same lady. I smiled and asked him, "Have you sung 'Come, Ye Disconsolate'?"

CHAPTER 13

Knowing What It Takes

OF COURSE, MUSIC MINISTRY ISN'T AS SIMPLE as picking the right hymns. Just as there is no "holy sound," there also is no "holy song list." Knowing what and why to sing is foundational, and inspiring the faithful to sing is critical, but actually getting people to sing is something else. It's where the rubber hits the road. The next couple of chapters will focus on this; thus, they will include some things that will be more addressed to my fellow musicians, but there is much for pastors and lay leaders to know about as well.

In my tradition, the word "cantor" denotes one whose role is to care for souls through the art of music. Cantors don't just sing or play or choose hymns; they oversee all aspects of the congregation's song. Thus, cantoral ministry goes beyond musical skill and encompasses a broad understanding of liturgy, hymnody, doctrine, theology, and worship practice. Even if you don't use the word "cantor" in your context, you should consider yourself a cantor for the purposes of this discussion if you are the primary person in your context who is responsible for congregational song.

But it isn't just cantors who shape the congregation's song. Pastors, other church workers, and lay leaders wield huge influence in the way they model congregational song and support and champion those who lead it. Material support is a key piece, of course, but supporting cantoral ministry entails much more than simply recruiting and paying musicians to make a joyful noise. It also entails understanding the essential elements of that noise so that all the leaders in a ministry context can better utilize and promote them.

What are those essential elements? In short: the primacy and clarity of melody, the unifying power of pulse, the essential energy of breath, and the roles of musical sounds in the various registers. These are the foundational paradigms for those who lead, sing, and play music for the congregation. As such, they should inform how the church discusses the art of music in worship, how the church's ensembles understand their work, and how the individual musicians develop their skills.

As for what is necessary to execute those elements, the one thing needful, of course, is the voice. When it comes to instruments beyond the voice, the better question is not "What is necessary?" but rather "How can instruments help rather than hinder the Lord's song?" There are essentially five ways, which can be covered by one to five musicians (or more), depending on their instruments, talent, sensitivity, and creativity: melodic guidance, harmonic comfort and color, bass momentum, rhythmic energy, and contrapuntal commentary.

1. **Melodic Guidance**. Because the Lord's song is word-driven, melody is the chief element and the most important thing to provide. If there is no instrument to supply the melody, it can be done by a singer or a choir. Instruments that play an octave higher than the congregation can provide additional help, as sounds in that register are more clearly heard over the congregation. A flute is ideal for this. Other instruments that can provide melodic guidance include

trumpets, recorders, pianos, and some synthesized sounds. Reed instruments matching the congregation's voices can help, too, as they cut through by virtue of their different timbres (clarinets, oboes, saxophones). Finally, the 4′ and 2′ stops on an organ sound one and two octaves higher than played. Someone with basic piano skill can also provide melodic guidance by playing an octave higher on the keyboard. So, with only a voice or a melodic instrument, melodic guidance can be provided.

2. **Harmonic Comfort and Color.** Taking into account the voices of the men, women, and children of the congregation, all of the singing occurs in a range of notes from nine or ten below middle C on the piano to nine or ten above. Sound in this range reinforces the singing, providing particular encouragement for those who sing little outside of church. Harmony played in this range increases the warmth of sounds and provides a comforting fullness to

the accompaniment. Harmonies played according to the logic of Western music theory also reinforce the direction of the melody. Harmony provides a range of colors that can help paint the text and deepen the people's understanding of, and connection to, the word. Harmonic instruments include the organ, piano, guitar, and accordion. This range can also be filled by brasses, strings, and winds through composed arrangements.

3. **Bass Momentum.** Whether or not percussion is used, bass instruments are best at clearly providing the pulse that drives and unites people in singing. Bass lines not only establish pulse; they maintain momentum and energy when providing fills between phrases or when elaborating on patterns used to establish pulse (sometimes referred to as "grooves"). Bass can be provided by the pedals on an organ or by a cello, piano, low brass such as a tuba, or a bass player. When a bass instrument is not available, this role of momentum

can be covered by a lower percussion instrument such as a djembe.

4. **Rhythmic Energy**. Pulse unites, and rhythm energizes. Rhythm can be filled in by rhythm guitar, piano, or well-articulated organ playing. It is also readily provided by percussion. Percussion instruments are powerful, so care needs to be used lest they overwhelm the melody. Remember: the song of the church is word-driven, not beat-driven. But even congregations that keep to traditional hymns, organ, and classical sacred music are thrilled by timpani. Generally, hand percussion is preferable to a drum set, as it is less likely to dominate the sound. That said, drum sets can be played in sensitive and supportive ways by the skilled player. But most drummers in North America have not had good models in this area but have instead been trained in beat-driven music. I experience the opposite in my work in Africa: when the drumming is on indigenous instruments such as the

tams (large drums played by hand), the playing is supportive of communal song. Yet, unfortunately, when imported drum sets are used (which happens more in the large cities), Western pop styles are often copied, and the congregation sings less as the sound overwhelms them.

5. **Contrapuntal Commentary**. When capable musicians are available, extra lines between phrases, counter-melodies, and descants can add a meaningful dimension, amplifying the message of a given stanza or adding heft to a refrain. Such can be added by any melodic instrument, by the organist, or by the pianist. Even percussion instruments can provide this in their own special ways. Care must be taken lest such spices overwhelm the dish, but when done well, the congregation savors the singing even more.

When the musicians of the parish are trained in these concepts, some remarkable things can begin to happen. An example from my own ministry is illustrative. While serving in a large congregation in Chicagoland, I had many resources, including a pipe organ, a grand piano, and two electronic keyboards: an electric piano and a synthesizer. It was an embarrassment of riches—but also an opportunity to teach. I had worked with teaching contemporary ensembles and praise bands the concepts of melody, harmony, bass, and rhythm before, but had yet to get to a point where an ensemble was really applying those ideas for the sake of the ministry.

Then, a keyboard ensemble I started at this congregation, whimsically named the Zebras (black and white keys, get it?), took hold of the concepts. I was inspired as they began to discuss among themselves how they would make ensemble for the sake of *leading the people in singing and using music to illustrate the texts*—a practice known as "text-painting"—*so as to inspire connections between the music and the words.*

It took a while to reach that level, but it was energizing to hear one keyboardist say, "Let me take the melody here so that I can use a trumpet sound to illustrate the call of God on this stanza," and then another reply, "Cool, I will leave the melody at that point and take the bass line you were playing." Whereupon yet another player suggested that she had a better bass sound to support a trumpet melody, resulting in a decision for a total switch-around between the four players on that stanza, as all understood the needs involved.

I want to note that when this group played, the service didn't become the Zebra service. Nor did the ensemble prepare any virtuosic special music. They were content to lead a hymn or two, a psalm, and/or a canticle. They didn't expect to run the whole service; they were simply one of the parish's musical groups that evoked melodies, enlarged the text, and supported a unifying rhythm so as to nurture the congregation's engagement with the Lord's song.

All of these same principles apply to the instrument most often used to lead congregational song, the organ. You may not use the "King of Instruments" at your church, but learning how it is best played is also illustrative of the common challenges we all have in leading worship music. Whatever instruments you may or may not use, the next chapter will point you to some helpful ways of thinking about church music and offer some tips that have proven helpful to many in a wide range of traditions.

CHAPTER 14

The King of Instruments

THE ORGAN HAS MANY MERITS FOR LEADING communal singing. The pipe organ, in particular, stands out, as it carries the significant benefit of wind moving through pipes— producing sound similarly to how the human voice moves air through vocal cords. There is no other single instrument so capable of leading a large number of human voices. And the text-painting capabilities of the "King of Instruments" are unquestionable.

Moreover, the pedals provide the bass that, when played well, helps unite the people in singing just as the bass player is the real timekeeper in a rock band. The manual keyboards offer a range of sounds, from flutes to strings to reeds, which allow for reinforcement in the singing range that comforts and encourages the singers and provide for melodic leadership as needed to guide them in the upper registers. Thus, with one capable musician, an organ can cover all the bases.

Still, the organ is only a tool. And, as a powerful one, it can do much damage as well as much good. Too often, it is played in ways that don't support the congregation's song. Remember, hymnody is not art music; it is folk song. If a congregation doesn't have the right hands to use this tool, it is better for them to be led by those who have developed talents on other instruments—including just using strong, capable voices to lead everyone a cappella. Though some believe they need to have an organ in order to sing hymns, psalms, and spiritual songs, Christians did fine without organs until a couple of centuries ago and, in many places, continue to do so. Similarly, though a standard four-piece rock band can also lead people capably, it is also something Christians have done—and continue to do—without.

The point is that instruments can be beneficial tools, but the only instruments that are necessary for worship are our voices. As for what people feel they *need* in order to worship, the only thing the bride of Christ truly needs is the bridegroom, who is the incarnate Word, not some holy sound of organs or rock bands.

Some might counter that the great, sturdy hymns of the Lutheran, Anglican, and Reformed traditions surely call for organs due to their more complex harmonic nature or the acoustics of many of the sanctuaries in which they are sung. I disagree. While it is certainly wonderful to sing our chorales with organs—at least good organs in the right hands—the singing should stand on its own.

Unfortunately, in many places, singing has become dependent on the organ. Rather than walking side by side, like two friends going to the store, the organist drags the congregation behind it (sometimes, it might be said, kicking and screaming). But the congregation should not be subserviently walking two paces behind, subserviently singing along. The congregation should actually not be dependent on instruments. If our hymnody is to remain a living tradition, it must maintain the character of folk song. Folk song enjoys accompaniment but can always stand on its own, a cappella.

As a missionary in francophone Africa, I have been pleased to share our living tradition of Lutheran folk song with brothers and sisters in

Christ who readily embrace Western hymnody and eagerly desire to learn more of it. Their instruments are not organs but drums and the occasional imported keyboard or bass guitar. Because their music is primarily lyrical, they readily learn and adopt our hymnody when it is taught to them as folk music, not art music. As such, they take the words, adapt the melodies to their musical language (changing a rhythm here or adding a note there), and then, as they make it their own, add percussion and establish their own, usually slower, tempo. This is as it should be: the people of God singing his song joyfully with the talents and resources they have. No organs, rock bands, or karaoke required!

In truth, the real "King of Instruments" is the one that we all have and are capable of using: the human voice. Where there is a voice, there is a song. The shy or insecure voice needs only another, more confident voice singing beside it to begin to find its own strength. Where there are no instruments, then, seek out the strong voices in your midst to help lead the singing. If there aren't strong voices, cultivate a few at a time, until you have the leaders you need and can begin to build a congregation of singers.

It's time for an important caveat. While fellow human voices provide the most encouraging sound, it is important to avoid overuse of microphones when you are utilizing song leaders. The pleasure of listening to good singers singing through microphones can cause congregations to quit singing and start listening, which is the opposite of what you want. So, if acoustics allow, avoid microphones altogether. But if you use them, do so sparingly— just enough to make the voices present in the room and no more. This has the added benefit of helping keep the other, supporting sounds from playing too loud.

Above all, the members of the congregation need to hear each other sing. If your worship space has poor acoustics for communal singing, designed more as an auditorium rather than a sanctuary, one inexpensive fix is to replace any absorbent acoustical tile with gypsum board. As good as your musicians may be, their efforts can be greatly frustrated by the room or the person running the soundboard. Indeed, whoever runs sound needs to understand the principles outlined earlier (melodic guidance, harmonic comfort and color, bass momentum, rhythmic energy, and contrapuntal commentary) so as to mix any amplification

accordingly. If the sound engineer does not understand that the people's voice—not the choir's or the
pastor's or a song leader's—should be the para-
mount sound in the mix, all of your best laid plans
can be compromised by one bad mix.

CHAPTER 15

Going to War with the Army You've Got

FOR THE MOST EFFECTIVE NURTURING OF CON-gregational song, the right kind of musicianship is essential. A particular combination of musicians, however, is not. As we have seen, the roles of bass, harmony, melody, and rhythm can be variously fulfilled according to the talents within each congregation. That means there are dozens of viable possibilities.

In one parish, for example, a skilled organist with a proper sensitivity toward congregational song may suffice well. In another, robust singing may be led by guitar, flute, accordion, and bass. Still another may have a pianist, a cellist, and a dedicated quartet of singers. A particular sound is not required—nor is it called for. What is needed is a sound that can lead, nurture, and energize the people in singing psalms, hymns, and spiritual songs. This may mean hiring someone from outside your congregation to fill a specific need. Most often, though, it means discovering the talent the Lord has already provided. Above all, we must avoid making idols out of past glories or human ideals and be willing to adapt when resources and talents change.

My fellow Lutheran cantor Stephen R. Johnson has stated this well:

> We Lutherans love our organ music, and rightly so. Hearing fine organ playing can be awe-inspiring. Parishes that have fine organs and organists to fully utilize them receive the great rewards that the instrument has to offer. The organ offers a panoply of colors, expressivity, and sensitivity in hymn accompanying, and of course, the great organ music of the Lutheran über-kantor—J. S. Bach. Bach has always been my favorite composer, long predating my years as a Lutheran, extending all the way back to my childhood. The more Bach I hear, the better …

The organ is a great instrument, and it is always wonderful to have a good organist. But if we do not have either, we as Lutherans may need to rethink our values. What makes Lutheran worship efficacious? Is it the organ, or is it the things that are played on the organ? Is it the chorale preludes of Bach? Or is it the chorales themselves, which place words and melodies on the lips and in the minds and hearts of parishioners for their spiritual nurturing? No chorale prelude can do that.

Is it possible that, without an organ at our disposal, we may need to be resourceful in finding ways to guide the congregation's song? Perhaps the use of a combination of instruments, or one or two good singers from the congregation, can accomplish this goal. Will it be as grandiose, as majestic? Probably not, but will it fulfill the admonition of Colossians 3:16 to "let the Word of Christ dwell richly in us?" Absolutely![28]

It is the hubris of our luxury in the United States to think that we *have* to have any instrument, frankly. Instruments have varied through the years, and the church's song has often flourished with none. In the medieval period, organs were primitive and fairly rare, used only for attendant music (prelude, gathering of offerings, communion distribution, postlude). The Renaissance composers focused on a pervasively vocal art. It was not until the Baroque period that we get a truly instrumental art that elevated the organ, with the great chorale preludes of Buxtehude, Pachelbel, and Bach, and even then, congregational song was often led by winds, strings, and choral voices. Only in the eighteenth century did the use of the organ to accompany congregational song become common practice. The people of God have sung his song for thousands of years, even back before the time of Moses, yet organs and other keyboard instruments have played a really significant role for, at most, the past four centuries.

And yet it is not uncommon today for churches who lack instruments to sing along with recorded music. While I do think such recordings are salutary for personal devotions, hospital visits, small group devotions, and the like, I think using karaoke elevates instrumental music and music preferences to a level they do not deserve. When such tracks are cued up on Sunday morning, the

message—however inadvertently communicated—
is this: "If we do not have instrumentalists, we
must use recordings because we cannot possibly
worship without them."

This attitude suggests there is something lacking in the congregation's song, that it is somehow
insufficient. Yet it is totally sufficient, for the Father
hears us through the ears of Jesus. He's not looking
for a concert. He delights in his children—just as a
mother delights in her toddler's crayon art and lovingly tapes it to the refrigerator. The tracks obscure
this. In using recorded music of any kind rather
than trusting their own voice, a congregation sub-
stitutes a purchased sacrifice of praise in place of
their own. One can fairly argue that such accompaniments are needed because the people don't know
this or that hymn, so I say, "Well, sing something
you know, then." God delights even in weak, struggling voices who humbly sing "Amazing Grace" or
"Jesus Loves Me" just as he loves the magnificent
praises heard at the Getty Sing! Conference. God
doesn't need us to bring in recordings so we can
sound better.

The authenticity of singing simple songs and
hymns is a far more convincing witness to those
who may come in or pass by, too. The visitor or

casual observer is going to be much more blessed by sincere and authentic singing than by a recording, whether or not it evokes a Nashville recording studio or Westminster Cathedral. Save the tracks for choir practice, if the song leaders need such help in learning to lead a song. But on Sunday morning, sing what the people can sing, using the talents the Lord has placed in the congregation for leading them.

Authenticity in worship will look and sound different in different places. Once, a pastor in Ontario approached me seeking help in keeping his congregation singing. One of the organists had died, and the other was from another town and only able to come every other week. The congregation had been using recorded organ music on the other Sundays, but they didn't care for the results. The flow of the service was often interrupted, the tempos were not sensitive to the assembly, and the sound of the majestic organ used in the recordings really didn't fit the room.

I asked the pastor if he had a choir, to which he chuckled a bit and said there had been a choir a few years ago, but how could they have a choir when they didn't have a music leader? I then clarified what I meant: not a choir to try to sing anthems or even liturgical music but simply people willing to help sing the hymns. I learned that there were a few strong voices the pastor thought would be willing to help, and that his wife had played flute in her high school band.

No further talent was discovered, but that was all that was needed. The solution was for the two men and three women with capable voices to form their choir. They would sit together every other week to provide a core sound to lead everyone in singing. They didn't learn parts; they just sang the melody. They needed only one rehearsal a month and used the recorded music to help them take to heart the hymns for the two services they would lead. The pastor's wife then added her flute. She would summon the hymns, playing the tune and thereby establishing their pulse and breath, and then the voices would lead. Flute came back in to highlight some stanzas, and the three forces of men's voices, women's voices, and flute were the functional equivalent of an organ leading the melody in multiple registers.

A few months later I touched base with the pastor, and he reported that it was going so well that the every-other-week organist had remarked that the congregation's singing had "never been better."

Such eclectic ensembles are the choice for some communities, even large congregations who are known for their strong singing. For example, at Capitol Hill Baptist in Washington, DC, with an attendance of nine hundred to one thousand people at the main service on Sunday morning, a robust song tradition has been led with a vocal quartet, acoustic piano, guitar, and, occasionally, cello. Former lead musician there Matt Merker trained his lead quartet to sing the first stanza with microphones and then back away, occasionally singing the second stanza at half-mic if the song is less familiar to the assembly. You can enjoy hymn festivals featuring strong congregational singing on their website.

Then there is Incarnate Word Lutheran Church, a mission congregation outside of Detroit. Though small, the congregation's song has been typically led by ensembles such as guitar, piano, oboe, flute, and violin. The worship is held at a local school, so there is no organ. No microphoned quartet is needed here, given the strength of the woodwind instruments to summon and guide melodies. Here, then, is another example of how many solutions there are for accompanying the Lord's song using a variety of talent. There are literally dozens of viable possibilities. All it takes is willingness, conviction, and effort.

However a congregation is led in the Lord's song, using the army you've got entails more than the tactics of how to lead the people in a given psalm or hymn. Once you get your people singing, it also means using your musicians to advance long-term strategic goals, such as nurturing a core group of hymns.

Repetition is the mother of learning, so disciplining the people into learning a set of songs by heart is an important part of cantoral ministry. Over time, this core should be shaped in a way that includes long-time favorites but also encompasses a repertoire that sings of the life of Christ, teaches the chief articles of faith, extols the sacraments, and provides comfort in times of trial. This is actually more of a challenge for congregations that are highly musically literate, as they tend to want to sing everything in the hymnal and are less comfortable with the repetition that leads to knowing hymns by heart.

This is where your team of musicians can be very helpful, as they can recapitulate your core hymns in creative ways throughout the church year so that they remain continually in the people's ears even as they don't necessarily sing them each time they are used. For instance, in addition to singing a certain hymn three or four times in a year, it may also be sung in a special arrangement by a soloist, sung another time as a choir anthem, played by a violin/piano duet on a different Sunday, and so forth. Team ministry can move this forward even further when key stanzas of the core hymns are quoted in sermons and in the prayers, taught in the Sunday school, and sung during congregational meetings.

I think all congregations should have about forty hymns they sing so often that the regulars know at least the first stanza by heart. Beyond that, there is a circle of adjacent texts (to the same tunes) and seasonal favorites that can pad that number up to about eighty to one hundred. Beyond that, some combination of high literacy and strong musicianship is needed to push that number much higher without leaving significant chunks of the congregation behind. It is better at that point to have a soloist or a choir sing those additional hymns as special music, perhaps with the congregation joining in the last stanza (or refrains, if the songs have them).

Finally, whatever troops you may have, enlist them into the teaching of new songs and the nurturing of core hymns. I mentioned earlier such tactics as lining out a new hymn. That can be step one, but with planning, it can even be better as step two. If possible, before the Sunday when the hymn is lined out for the people to sing the first time, have a choir or a soloist sing it first. Over the weeks where the song is being introduced, work the tune into the attendant music of the service—preludes, voluntaries, music during distribution. These are moments when different instruments are particularly helpful because layers add interest.

Then, depending on the difficulty level of the hymn and the literacy level of the congregation, when the congregation sings the hymn the second time (when it is not lined out beforehand), have a choir or soloist take part in the hymn, both for the sake of giving the people additional hearings but also by heightening interest in the hymn through the variety. An easier hymn tune may just need a clear intro and a soloist singing the first stanza, after which all can join in. A more challenging one may be best served by a full instrumental introduction, choir on stanza 1, soloist on stanza 2 (again, layers maintain interest!), the whole congregation trying it for stanza 3, duet or different soloist on stanza 4 (allowing people to hear it again and process it), and then all again for stanza 5.

Along the way, as you employ all the talents of your people, people will increasingly gain appreciation of the gift of the Lord's song. They will love it more and more as the word dwells in them richly. They will also value it more because the church leadership clearly values it. The adage is true, "If it is important to you, it's important to them." As with most things in life, you get what you work for. Remember the parable of the talents (Matt 25:14–30; Luke 19:11–27). If you invest what the Lord has given you in your congregation, you will receive more. Congregations that worship well attract more who love the Lord's appearing. But if you don't use the army the Lord has given you, don't expect any return—and don't be surprised if the Lord takes those talents from you.

CHAPTER 16

Don't Be a Hero

WE ALL HAVE DIFFERENT TALENTS, WHETHER in the areas of math, language, art, building, or something else, and God has given us neighbors to bless by using those talents. This chapter will focus on developing one's musical talent, but even if you aren't a musician, there will still be something here for you because everyone has some kind of talent.

God gives us our talents to share, not hoard, so it follows that the key to effective church musicianship is to play outside of oneself. This means having a continual awareness of those you are playing for, whether they are being called to listen or to participate.

Rather than playing music in one's personal universe—like the archetypal artist celebrated during the Romantic era and upheld today in so much popular culture—the cantoral musician plays for and with the people. Instead of expressing a personal vision and inviting others to join that vision, he or she seeks to manifest what God has already done, reveal his creative activity, and give expression to the experience of faith. Rather than saying, "Come into my world," the cantor says, "Come into God's world"; rather than "Look at what I have done," the cantor says, "Look what God has done"; and rather than "Behold my experience and feelings," the cantor shares life in Christ and says, "Come, let us sing of this life we share." Thus, the cantor ministers not through an idealized art that stands on its own without an audience but through a practical art that depends on its hearers—both when they are summoned to hear and when they are summoned to join in singing.

At church music workshops, I sometimes take time to talk about my favorite organist. You might think he or she would be someone of great name recognition and renown, at least among those who know and play the instrument. Instead, I enjoy revealing that he is a friend of mine who is a retired engineer. Tom only had a few years of lessons in his childhood, and he doesn't even own a pair of organ shoes (he plays barefoot). He was one of the regular organists at the congregation I served for many years in Chicagoland, where we had four services each weekend in addition to a couple of chapel services each week.

You might be wondering why my favorite organist is not a virtuoso but someone who has only had a few years of formal study. The answer? Tom doesn't box outside his weight. If you are around when Tom plays, you will not hear him stumble through a fancy prelude beyond his skill level or take on a hymn accompaniment that overtaxes his technique. Instead, Tom plays consistently singable tempos, uses clear registrations, gives predictable breath cues, and maintains the pulse between stanzas. In other words, everyone can sing with Tom. Why? Because he listens to the assembly and plays to accompany their singing. God be praised! If only we could say the same about many a more highly trained organist.

This outward focus aligns with the spirituality of vocation taught by Martin Luther. Emphasizing that every Christian is a royal priest (1 Pet 2:9) while upholding the distinctive role of the pastoral office (Acts 20:28; 1 Tim 3; Titus 1:5), Luther showed how God uses all Christians to accomplish his will and work in the world. Grounding his teaching in the recovered gospel of the Reformation, with its emphasis on salvation by grace alone through faith alone—and not through the merits of offerings and works—he elevated the daily work of all believers to the same rank as those called to serve as pastors, his under-shepherds.

With the worship service understood as a Divine Service wherein God serves his people rather than a means by which man gains merit, ministers are seen by Luther as no more priestly than the rest of us. The work of the Lord's ministry through his word by preaching and sacrament is seen as the inauguration of God's kingdom—a kingdom "not of this world" (John 18:36). Yet at the same time, God still rules over the nations through temporal authorities. Luther described this dichotomy as two realms or "kingdoms." Using two hands to illustrate the two kingdoms, Luther explained that God works spiritually by his word with his right hand, and temporally with his left hand to maintain outward peace and social order by means of secular powers. Because all work serves others, it is seen as holy work, no matter which kingdom it is in.

Accordingly, in his Small Catechism, Luther replaced the whole Roman system of holy orders

with a "Table of Duties" that describes how all
Christians have holy work to do. God calls upon
us to love others regardless of their citizenship
in heaven (Matt 22:37–40; Mark 12:29–31; Luke
10:26–28). God doesn't need our works, Luther
said, but our neighbor does.[29] Yet as Jesus said, "As
you did it to one of the least of these my brothers, you did it to me" (Matt 25:40). In serving our
neighbor, we bless the Lord.

This is essential to understanding how the
work of the musician—or the butcher or baker or
candlestick maker—takes on a different character
when carried out with an evangelical attitude. This
reformation of vocation had a powerful impact:
no longer was God's work confined to the sanctuary, the monastery, or the nunnery; instead, God's
work was understood to be done through every
Christian as we live the Christian life.

This doctrine of vocation comes radically into
play in the duties of the church musician, as the
ministry of music works dynamically in both the
temporal and spiritual realms. Remember how
we have not yet heard the holy sound? Though
the proclamation of the word is wholly a spiritual matter, its activity through music takes place
for now through worldly means. This is why this

outlining of church musicianship relates to all vocations. Until the trumpet sounds and the last day comes, we are all in the world but not of it (John 17:14–18).

Applying this doctrine to the vocation of church musician, one sees that rather than seeking to produce a powerful internal experience or achieve a magnificent realization of notes on a page, the cantor seeks to engage the hearers in their situation. This may seem to increase the pressure to perform, but it actually takes the pressure off. Yes, some congregants are tough customers. But unlike the entertainer or classical artist, the church musician does not need to impress. When the focus is outward, the ear is tuned toward the congregation and the mind is able to let go of details that don't serve that focus. Yes, skill is required, but the goal is not ultimately to perform. Instead, the goal is to communicate melody, cue breathing, establish pulse, and maintain line. All of these tasks can and should be accomplished within the musician's capabilities, at whatever level he or she plays.

Yes, a certain amount of skill needs to be developed in each of these areas—a considerable amount, indeed, when one musician is called to cover all the bases on one instrument. But once someone is able to deliver melody in rhythm, the essentials are there, leading to the ability to let go in performance and engage with the assembly. Nothing comes out of one's instrument that one hasn't put into it, so practice is essential to musicianship, but one should not distract oneself from the song while leading it. The clever harmony or counterpoint you may have practiced but are not yet comfortable to execute can wait for some other time!

This view of spirituality in vocation is referred to by theologians as *extra nos*, Luther's term for "outside of us." This understanding points both to how God in Christ comes to us externally through means but also how we glorify God through means as well. While certainly God created us as sentient beings and called everything he makes—including our minds and feelings—good (Gen 1:31), he is not served through the loftiness of our thoughts and the depths of our emotions. He desires mercy from us, just as he is faithful and merciful, slow to anger, and abounding in steadfast love. What we do, then, with our thoughts and feelings is, in the end, much more important than having them.

I highlight this again because it runs counter to how so many view the work of musicians and the role of music. Even if you don't share this view of Christian spirituality, it is important for you to understand how this view of vocation informs the craft of the cantor. Just as Jews demanded signs and the Greeks sought wisdom (1 Cor 1:22), so today audiences crave amazing performances or exquisite art music. Both miss the mark when it comes to music ministry, even as in many quarters impressive shows are well-received. For the cantor's music is not for the cantor but for the congregation.

Remember Veith's pop-folk-art continuum? It comes into play again here. Going too far to one side risks slipping into *traditionalism*, what the theologian Jaroslav Pelikan called "the dead faith of the living," as opposed to *tradition*, the "living faith of the dead."[30] Going too far to the other side risks sliding into emotionalism, which confuses faith with depth of feeling rather than enjoying the feelings that spring from faith. As mentioned before, there is room for music that tilts to either side, but the grounding must be in the center, where the assembly is intrinsically connected to song by virtue of sharing its heritage. Popular accessibility and artistic beauty have their place, but sacred song is rooted in the cultural inheritance of the church, which flows from the word of God. It is not properly rooted in a musical universe created by the composer or the feelings expressed by a performer.

This same *extra nos* sensitivity is vital in the planning of worship as well. Pastors, elders, and worship committees who share the duties of hymn, psalm, and spiritual song selection need to have the same rootedness in the same inheritance. Just as church musicians can make the mistakes of programming their favorites without due concern for the congregation, the same dynamic is at play with others involved in this task. This is understandable. Music is a powerful tool, and the Spirit uses the word magnified through song to great benefit. Thus, musicians and non-musicians alike often come to the worship-planning table with great zeal for sharing the soundtrack of their personal experiences of the faith, assuming that the same great things will happen for the congregation if only they get to hear the same music.

While this is indeed a great temptation for new church musicians, it tends to play out even more in the ideas of pastors, elders, and congregation members. It is vital, then, for all who make decisions in this area to understand this temptation, accept that others will not necessarily respond to music in the same way, and accept better criteria for song selection than their own personal experience.

This understanding, once gained, is liberating for worship planners. Rather than trying to craft *impactful* worship services (which opens the door to worship becoming the scapegoat for any shortfalls in ministry goals), they can relax. Instead of making an idol of either popularity or correctness, they can let go of the burden of their own thoughts and feelings and give it over to the Holy Spirit. Cantoral ministry trusts that the Spirit is at work in the word, alive in the body of Christ, sanctifying that body according to God's promise. As a result, it grounds worship planning on how best to deliver the gifts of God to the people of God, trusting that, through the word, God will accomplish his purposes (Isa 55:11).

All of this doesn't mean you get to mail it in, of course. If anything, the preceding discussion should highlight the holiness of cantoral ministry and the seriousness with which it should be approached. But realizing that our work is not truly ours but the Lord's does have profound implications on how we plan, prepare, and practice. As we do all of those things, we must always seek to look *extra nos*—outside of ourselves—and not be surprised when the result is not what we might have expected.

Here's an illustration from an organist workshop I led a few years ago. As is my practice, I was strongly encouraging the organists to begin their work on a hymn *away from the organ* by standing and singing the tune. This is so the musician can ascertain a tempo for the song that allows for proper breathing to prepare and sustain phrases while maintaining steadiness of pulse. Tempi that are too fast may maintain a phrase without allowing enough time to breathe; tempi that are too slow may allow time to breathe but drag phrases out beyond breath capacity. (There are other reasons this practice is commendable, but this is the goal I was working on at the time.)

As I was presenting this concept, one of the organists in the class raised her hand to affirm what I was saying about the importance of breath. However, what she shared was a classic case of right problem, wrong solution. She gave the example of a hymn on which it is indeed a challenge to find a good tempo and then reported that she slowed down at the end of every phrase to give people time to breathe. The real problem, though, was that her tempo was too fast, evidenced by her bending the time so people could breathe. Her approach solved the breath problem but created another: by compromising the beat, she was robbing the music of the uniting power of pulse. This made the assembly entirely reliant on her in order to stay together, sapping the hymn of energy.

Rather than engage in a debate or tell her she was wrong, I created an experience that helped her and others find a better way. I had the twenty or so of us that were there stand and form a line. We then sang the whole hymn—all five stanzas—while walking. We snaked our way from the conference room down a hall into the sanctuary and then out the sanctuary back to the conference room. By the second stanza, we had settled into a tempo we kept for the rest of the hymn—one that did not need to be bent to breathe. (Note: the tempo was not determined by the tempo of our initial pace, but the walking freed us from the page so that we were able to find a more natural singing tempo as the ideal pace comes to align with the pairing of movement and voice.)

After the exercise, the organist was ecstatic. She had never done anything like that before, and she reported that she had already marked that tempo down with the metronome app on her phone. Smiles abounded. Such is the payoff when one steps away from the ruts of learning notes or the demands of performing and does the work of considering how best to lead the people in singing the Lord's song.

Whether you are the musician or the pastor, you don't have to be a hero. God is already our hero. Yours is the honor of being his ambassador, sharing the good news he has given you to share. Your congregation doesn't have to be heroes either. Though you should cultivate the Lord's song and joyfully employ your talents and tongues to sing his praise, there is no artistic standard or level of singing your congregation needs to attain for his will to be done. God is faithful. Trust him, for "he will surely do it" (1 Thess 5:24).

CHAPTER 17

Summoning the Song

THE CHIEF MUSICIAN AND THOSE UNDER HIS direction need to do more than skillfully accompany the people in holy song. When I had the organists at my workshop walk while singing to find the right tempo for the hymn, the exercise bore fruit because the musicians involved shared a strong familiarity with the tune. They weren't glued to a page, sight-reading a hymn, but were able to get their heads out of the score, engage their bodies, and move through the piece holistically. Such possibilities increase over time according to the *habitus* of the cantor. As Harold Senkbeil explains in the seminal work of this Care of Souls series,

> Every useful human endeavor is more than just mastering external skills; these flow from an inner attitude or aptitude

developed by repetition. By practicing for years a musician grows not only in instrumental proficiency, but in the artistic expression that informs reliably fine performances. A chef's expertise isn't merely a matter of external technique, but the internal intuition that results from years of habitually blending the right ingredients, timing, temperature, seasoning, and presentation that makes for consistently fine cuisine … [and] a farmer learns his craft over time and experience as he is shaped by the very crops and animals he tends and harvests.[31]

Habitus nurtures intimate familiarity with the song repertoire of the congregation. It allows the cantor to gain continual insights into the dimensions of the texts and tunes, opening up avenues by which he can engage the congregants under his care with the Lord's song. It guides him in discerning good ways to involve the different voices and instruments in the congregation and gives insight into the kinds of music by which the talents under his care can most effectively magnify and proclaim the word of God. This extends significantly to the composing and arranging work of the cantor, as he crafts music to match the abilities and styles of the parish musicians—or finds arrangements in the marketplace that fit his people and serve the congregation well.

Many places do not have a cantor or even a capable part-time music director. This means that the role of summoner is often taken up by the pastor—whether he likes it or not. In this case, he becomes the de facto chief musician. But whoever fills this role, whether a professional church musician leading a sizeable music ministry or a pastor leading hymns in a small congregation, should develop the *habitus* of a song leader. This involves signaling a good key for the assembly, establishing tempo, cueing breath, and being sensitive to when one's voice or instrument is needed more and when it is best to back away. These skills are most certainly developed over time and come from having your congregation's repertoire of the Lord's song in your own heart. As I heard Russian pianist Vladimir Feltsman say at a master class once, "You can't give away something you don't have."

Even after years of leading congregational song, I still must return to these basics. A few years ago, an experience at a parish in Oklahoma where I was serving reminded me yet again of the need to practice what I preach.

I have liked the Michael Joncas song "Take and Eat" ever since I found it in the hymnal supplement of the Wisconsin Evangelical Lutheran Synod. You can also find it in the latest editions of the GIA hymnal *Gather*, and there are several recordings on YouTube of various quality, instrumentations, and tempi. I've always wanted a congregation to embrace it, but my attempts to minister to people with the song had fallen flat. I had started to wonder if this was a song I liked but that I really shouldn't impose on the people. Even though the words were good, maybe I liked the chord progression too much or the melody wasn't one they could embrace.

But as I prepared worship for this particular Sunday in Oklahoma, the appointed readings motivated me to try it one last time. I approached the hymn anew and did *exactly what I teach others to do but had failed to do myself*. I got up from the piano and sang the song *unaccompanied*. I memorized the lyrics and mused on them. I sang the song in the sanctuary, imagining people in the pews and considering how I might bring these words of our Lord alive in their ears. I spent an hour doing this on Friday at church, another half hour on Saturday, and another half hour on the piano at home Saturday night. In other words, I did everything I should have done previously with the song in order to prepare to *minister* through this music.

By the time we sang the third refrain Sunday morning, I could tell that something was different in the room. By the final refrain, the sanctuary was filled with singing—the kind of heartfelt singing I had always hoped for but had previously failed to elicit with this song. It was a perfect moment, extraordinarily delightful and beautiful. This was not the manipulation of emotions such as entertainers seek but the extraordinary delight Christians share when the music succeeds in joining the people's voice to the word of God. Making this connection is the duty of the church musician. When we succeed, people are connected to and comforted by the promises of Jesus.

The "magic" moment of singing "Take and Eat" that morning in Oklahoma came about not because I was into the song or because of some inner feeling I had. That kind of playing and singing might provide an inspirational testimony, but the hearers remain passive. It can even devolve into entertainment. No, this result happened because I had consciously moved outside of myself and worked on singing the song with the intention of inviting those present to join in singing the Lord's song. I won't say how it was different—faster or slower, louder or softer—lest the reader draw the wrong conclusions. It's not a matter of tempo or dynamics, though they are part of the equation. It has instead to do with the fundamentals of breath and line and how both the energy of breath and engagement of line depend on the musician being connected to the hearers in order to be effective. Thus, the answers depend on the size and quality of the room, the number of hearers, and the capabilities of the musician's instrument(s). They are acquired through the *habitus* of the chief musician, a *habitus* which is insufficient for church music unless the musician deliberately considers the assembly he is called to lead.

The discipline I just described flows from the essence of musicianship—and the particular kind of musicianship it takes to lead congregational song. As important as notation is, the page just contains symbols. Those who lead worship music need to get past the notes on the page and discover the music the notation signifies. Notes and words and rhythms are but the beginning of true practicing. If you stop there, you'll miss the music, and the result will be similar to that of a pastor dryly reading his sermon rather than really preaching it to you.

So, approach each song as if it were a little sermon. Focus not just on what you are singing but seek to look beyond the page to *whom you are singing it with and for.* In this way, the ultimate goal of your music-making will not be to express yourself or recapitulate some idealized, correct performance but to confess Christ, wherein God's magic happens as he has his way with us through the rich indwelling of the word.

This magic can also be illustrated by a couple of extraordinary delights I enjoyed at the National March for Life I attended a few years ago in Washington, DC. The first was an uplifting experience jamming with some street musicians I encountered as I exited the metro on my way up to the National Mall. They were singing "This Is the Day," and, moved by their enthusiasm, I asked to join in on the keyboard. At that point, the pianist shifted to singing more harmony and adding some handclapping behind his fellow singer. We segued into "What a Mighty God We Serve" and drew a small crowd of onlookers. Eventually a video someone had taken made the rounds on social media and got a lot of views in Lutheran circles. One might wonder how such an impromptu performance relates to the cultivated leadership I just described, so bear with me.

Some responded to the video at the time, knowing my preference for chorales over popular genres of Christian music, and asked why I seemed to enjoy the jam session so much. Fair question, especially given my position that the song of the church should be word-driven, not beat-driven. I could respond by noting this musical interlude wasn't part of the Divine Service, but even though that's an important point, the answer is not that simple.

Ultimately the question misses the mark because the issue is not one of style. Even as I think that there are some musical choices that are not in good order and that the church is best served by "well-regulated" church music (to borrow a phrase from Bach), I don't think there is anything inherently wrong with hand-clapping or even dancing during worship—*when it is real.* And by "real" I don't mean whether people are *feeling it* or not, because any half-decent musician can whip up emotions and get the poorly catechized to think they are in the Spirit. What I am referring to is the reality of manifesting the faith God gives to us as brothers and sisters in Christ. That's something we can judge objectively.

When music is real—when it is faithful—it is reverent and authentic. To be reverent means that it honors God, acknowledges God, and is focused on God. This is much more easily done in cultures with histories of rhythmic music and ceremonial dance, such as I live among when I am in Africa. This leads to the second point: authenticity. If I am in a community that sings jubilantly with percussion instruments to organically proclaim the steadfast love of the Lord, then there is no distraction or manipulation. But where such music is not part of the culture, it is, at best, merely entertainment, often distracting from the gospel and manipulating emotions rather than giving voice to our shared experience of the faith.

How can one tell the difference? It's pretty easy. *If you are the music or song leader, drop out.* If the community owns the song, the musician who summoned the song can step away and the song will go on. I knew the refrain to "Take and Eat" would have gone on that day in Oklahoma even had I dropped out. Indeed, as those in the congregations

I have served well know, I often do drop out, and those moments are often the most magical.

This is not about style but about a musicianship that grows out of a common culture and connects with the community called to sing together. Music promulgated in the name of entertainment evangelism, sometimes called "the attractional model," fails this test no matter how professionally it is done and no matter how many in the congregation emote along with the singer or enjoy the sound of the band. Such music in the assembly's stead, with the volume turned up so that the impression of great worship is created, is artificial.

By contrast, the sound of Lutherans in Pointe-Noire, Congo, chanting the Lord's Prayer or midwestern Anglicans singing a setting of an ancient hymn of praise, the Te Deum, a cappella in four-part harmony is truly authentic. Both instances are about the joyful noise of God's people singing together.

That said, I certainly do see a role of musical testimony that edifies a congregation and broadens their repertoire. Some will inevitably be entertained by that—whether one powerfully presents a Renaissance motet or an African hymn. But that is a matter of catechesis. Once a congregation gets used to owning their role in worship, they'll clap no more for the music than they do for the sermon—or for receiving the sacrament. (Seriously, if applause in church is really directed to God, why don't people clap after receiving the Lord's Supper?)

As a final example, another event at that same March for Life helped me to realize the high delight of sharing what we have taken to heart. As I made my way up Constitution Avenue toward the US Supreme Court with thousands of others, I found myself singing hymns a cappella with students from a Lutheran high school in Missouri, and the experience reminded me yet again of how important it is for Christians to own their song. One is hard-pressed to open hymnals or song sheets on a long, cold march with a huge crowd. Thankfully, with this group, such was not needed. These teenagers knew multiple stanzas of many classic hymns, from Lutheran chorales such as "Now Thank We All Our God"[32] and "A Mighty Fortress Is Our God" (Luther's original, rhythmic version)[33] to ecumenical standards such as "Holy, Holy, Holy"[34] and "I Know that My Redeemer Lives."[35]

Sure, sometimes someone stumbled on a word or two, including me, but there were always several who could keep it going, so we helped each other as we went along our way. We also took turns summoning the hymns, including some common liturgical songs we all knew, such as "Create in Me a Clean Heart, O God"[36] or one of the Agnus Dei settings from our *Lutheran Service Book*. The song flowed from our hearts, and it was real. There was no organ, no band, no karaoke machine required, just Christians summoning and encouraging one another in the Lord's song.

Sadly, most teenagers today don't know these songs. Even most Christian teenagers would be hard-pressed to sing more than maybe a stanza of "Silent Night" or "Amazing Grace." This is why they need other generations to teach them (Ps 78:4) and why we all need to teach and encourage one another (Eph 5:19). As the late writer and theologian Marva Dawn taught so well, "The young need the songs of the old and the old need the song of the young."[37] We are indeed better together.

Yet communal singing—one of the most unifying experiences humankind has ever known, one that was embraced by the church and by which the people of God have been known for millennia—has in large part been set aside. We need to find our voice again, for the sake of the world.

It begins with you. It doesn't matter if you and your people can only sing a dozen (or fewer) songs unplugged, and it doesn't mean you should always sing unplugged (though those from a cappella traditions who are reading this will affirm the power of which I'm speaking). Start from there and build a core of songs you can truly sing together. Then add half a dozen each year until you get to around forty or fifty. Such is enough. One can and should sing other things around that core, using hymn books or bulletins or screens as needed, but having a core that is known by heart is essential to having a singing community.

This core, of course, should be appropriate to one's context, one's traditions, and, of course, one's theology. Yet we should be sure also not to all be in our own bubbles. We are the church, after all, the body of Christ across space and time. So it is important to balance local needs and theological commitments with the universality or catholicity of the church. If you are non-denominational, include enough ecumenical hymnody that your people will have core connections should they move. If you are in a denomination, be mindful of what you share with the congregations you walk alongside, even as you include some local favorites.

Whatever you are singing, make sure you are summoning the folk music of your people. Keep it real. Don't substitute someone else's joy for your own. There's no reason for it even if you think you are doing it for the young or for the seekers. The truth is that you'll never be as convincing singing someone else's song as you will be singing your own. Again, per Feltsman, you can only give away what you have.

As the cantor is in tune with the congregation's repertoire, and as the ministry team shepherds the singing, the role of summoning takes another form: evoking a common text for mutual meditation. Once people know songs, or at least parts of songs, by heart, one is able to richly minister to them through the attendant music as well as through the song singing. Rather than just establishing a mood as the people gather, give offerings, receive communion, or come to the altar, the power of melody can be employed to bring the words of psalms, hymns, and spiritual songs to mind. The common song is reinforced, and its power to bring spiritual peace, comfort, and cheer is further unleashed.

Finally, I believe it is our duty, as leaders of the church's song, to shape the congregation's song over time so that its repertoire offers a full witness of Scripture—singing of the life of Christ, God's fulfillment of his promises through him, how he continues to bless us in the present age, and the life of the world to come. "I will sing of the steadfast love of the LORD, forever; with my mouth I will make known your faithfulness to all generations. For I said, 'Steadfast love will be built up forever; in the heavens you will establish your faithfulness' " (Ps 89:1–2). We are called to sing the whole story of God's love, and we joyfully sing it together as the people of God (Jer 33:11).

This means singing of his salvation from beginning to end and, inasmuch as it can be done naturally and authentically, embracing the song of the whole church—not just one or two favored musical styles. A repertoire that embraces plainsong ("O Come, O Come, Emmanuel"),[38] chorales ("A Mighty Fortress Is Our God"),[39] hymns ("Holy, Holy, Holy"),[40] metric psalms ("O God, Our Help in Ages Past"),[41] gospel songs ("The Old Rugged Cross"),[42] global music ("Holy Spirit, the Dove Sent from Heaven"),[43] and modern hymns ("In Christ Alone")[44] connects the singers with the universality of the church and confesses the oneness we share in the Christ we have sung throughout the ages.

It also affirms the various generations and sub-cultures within a congregation rather than confining the singing to the limits of a particular style or two. In this way, one not only avoids falsely upholding one kind of music as the holy sound, one also gains a bold confession of the church's oneness in every time and place. There is a tension in this, as the need for embracing a core set of songs limits their number, while the breadth of the church and the depth of the scriptural witness inspire a countless number of songs. Discernment is required, including wisdom to know when something isn't working or when a song needs to be retired (if only for a season).

But take heart: such deep thinking about congregational song is worth the investment. As your people sing more richly of God's love and experience the dynamics of how his word intersects with the music of his people, they will develop more and more taste for such rich fare. Even those who rarely sing outside of church will come to rejoice in the blessing of the Lord's song and consider it their own.

Comfort and Joy

As a leader of any kind in the church, your leadership is ultimately a spiritual leadership. As such, it is tethered to the Lord of the church himself, Jesus Christ of Nazareth, the Son of God, begotten of the Father before all worlds. He is the Vine, and we are the branches (John 15:5–8).

The wisdom to discern authenticity and your motivation to summon the song come from the Holy Spirit. As in all forms of ministry, if you rely on your own wisdom and strength to make ministry happen, you will soon find yourself depleted of spiritual energy and, in the end, physically and emotionally drained as well. Whatever role you play in singing faith into human hearts, you need to be hearing the Savior's song for you. He gives you a song, too. And over and over, he provides in that song the inspiration you need to inspire others.

Listening to Jesus' singing requires filtering out a lot of noise. Our postmodern world is a hectic place, both externally and internally. Around us we have the hustle and bustle of modern lives, such as most of our parents and grandparents have had. Even on the modern farm, life is not so simple as it once was. But the twenty-first century has added an internal hustle-bustle: the internet. It's hard to tune it all out and not be an information glutton. Noise within and noise without mirror two of the errors worship music can fall into: the impressive style and brilliant show of entertainment and the soothing yet deceiving chords of mysticism. The former mirrors the diversions of the world; the latter the numbing distractions of our own minds.

This is not to say that impressive musician-ship or soothing harmonies are in themselves bad things. But the emphases of entertainment evange-lism on polish and show, and of charismatic music on beautiful, mystic repetition, make music itself—rather than the word of God—the primary thing. Listening to music in this way misses hearing the voice of Jesus. Those who want their hearers to hear Jesus singing need to cultivate listening habits themselves so that they are attuned to the living voice of the gospel. This entails improving listening skills and practicing discernment in one's listening habits. Let me offer a few practical suggestions that I hope will help you do this.

First, remember that the Sabbath was made for man, not man for the Sabbath. Therefore, take time to listen to the songs that will be sung at church the following Sunday. Listen to the words and be mindful of them. Maybe you don't have time to listen to everything each week. But you may find this practice such a blessing that you will make more time for it as you go along.

For starters, pick one hymn or song and let the word of God dwell in you richly as you hear it. Listen to what Jesus is saying through this word magnified. (Of course, if the song doesn't really magnify the word, then it's time to think more critically about its value, right?)

If you are in a tradition that makes use of instrumental music, have the band, the pianist, or the organist record one of their selections for you. Make sure you know the text associated with whatever melody is featured in the instrumental piece, and then practice listening to the piece. Allow the text to come to you slowly and listen for how the instrumental music paints and supports the melody and, thus, the text. (And if there is no hymn, psalm, or spiritual song associated with the melody, then please have your musicians read this book.)

Another tip is to unplug and go for a walk or simply sit in a chair, maybe with a cup of coffee, and let any hymn you love have its way with you. Take some time to reconnect with how much you love it and remember the first time you heard it or came to appreciate it. Maybe you've forgotten some of the words and would benefit from looking them up. Maybe you'll be motivated to find a fresh recording on the internet when you plug back in. Or perhaps you will share the joy you've recovered with a friend or family member. You can't really give away joy you don't have. Take time to rejoice in your salvation and, in turn, you will find yourself better helping your community make a joyful sound.

In addition, renew your mind and learn some of the worship songs by heart, even if just a couple of hymn stanzas or song refrains. There is a rich tradition of Christian meditation on the word that includes memorizing devotional texts. If this is new to you, start small. Don't expect to be a champion at this sort of thing like Ed Nalle, the lead singer

from the Christian vocal group Glad, who effort-
lessly recites entire chapters of Pauline Epistles.
Remember, you don't need to be a hero. But you
do need to be in the word. Let the word dwell
within you so richly that you can look away from
the hymnal or the screen and sing right to and with
your fellow believers. The blessings will abound.

Take every opportunity, also, to go to church
yourself without being a leader. One of the health-
iest things I see my pastor doing when it is the vic-
ar's turn to preach is delegating the pastoral role
to another pastor for one of the services so that
he can just sit in a pew with his family and worship. Similarly, I, as a church musician, experience
growth when others lead the music and I get to
sing with the assembly.

For both pastors and my fellow cantors, this is
not always so easy. While one would expect church
workers to be very good at sitting still in the pew
and reverently soaking it all in, many are quite
fidgety. I think it is because one loses a bit of the
habitus of the *churchgoer* when one is always the
church-doer. Yes, we still worship and receive God's
gifts while we lead our services, but there is considerable truth to how one can only really worship
when one steps back and lets others do the serving.

Finally, pray. Pray for those who will come to worship as well as for yourself and others who will lead in various ways—from assisting ministers to acolytes to ushers to musicians. Take time to pray a psalm that will be part of the service. Let the words of that psalm inspire your heart to pray for related concerns for yourself and all involved.

One helpful tip with some psalms is to change the pronoun so that you can pray that text about someone else or for a group. For example, change the voice from first-person singular to third-person singular, and pray Psalm 26 as you have in mind a soloist who will be singing the following Sunday: "Lord, she loves the habitation of your house, and the place where your glory dwells. Do not sweep her soul away with sinners, nor her life with bloodthirsty men, in whose hands are evil devices, and whose right hands are full of bribes. But as for her, she shall walk in her integrity; in the great assembly she shall bless the LORD."

In all these ways, you will be prepared to support your congregation in a repertoire of Christ-centered songs and hymns. Experiencing the comfort and joy of the Lord's song yourself, you will find no lack in your ability to share the glad tidings of the gospel.

CHAPTER 19

The Art of Listening

THE INTENTIONAL PREPARATION SUGGESTED
in the last chapter should line up with the songs and
hymns of the congregation you serve. Presuming
you are taking to heart the same music your congregation is singing, you will grow together as
more move from just singing along to joyfully
participating. Just as the people of Israel understood the Lord's song as their song, so, too, will
your congregation identify with it. Music played
for them—rather than music played *at* them (which
happens in both congregations with modern worship bands and congregations featuring classical
sacred music)—will lead them to understand
church music as their music. The joyful participation which follows then leads them to embrace
the Lord's song as their own anthem. In doing so,

the great exchange of Christ's life for ours is manifested and magnified.

As you reflect on the progress you are making, take time to note each Sunday how the people sang. Though what is sung is of primary importance, the goal, after all, is for people to sing it. Discuss with others how they thought things went, and be honest. Criticism need not necessarily mean a bad choice was made, and it can help you understand how to do better. And, yes, it can also save you from repeating mistakes! As Keith Getty says, the question we should ask after church is not "How did we do?" but "How did the people sing?"[45]

This often means, once you get the singing going, not singing yourself. I know it's hard ("How Can I Keep from Singing," right?), but you can't really say how the people sang if you don't listen to them. The ultimate goals of cantoral ministry are achieved only when the chief musician is actively listening to the congregation. Just as the seasoned choir director does not sing along with his choir but models for them and then serves as their first audience and primary receiver and encourager of their sound, so does the cantor model for the congregation and then actively engage his ears to the sounds of the assembly. In response to what is heard, the chief musician must diagnose and apply the help needed to encourage and nurture the singers and their song. The benefits are both temporal and spiritual.

The centrality of the people's song leads to an important corollary: be careful with special music. While certainly gospel proclamation in song, skillfully played and sung, can be a great blessing, it also draws musical creativity and energy—as well as congregational time—away from communal singing of the Lord's song. Many a congregation has suffered in worship as the church's musicians put excessive efforts into concert series and special programs.

This can happen even when too much time is spent on special pieces for Sunday morning. In all our musical choices, we must ask, "What would we do if we did not do this?" Many great ideas fail this test in favor of *just* singing something the congregation knows and loves (which, hopefully, will increasingly be the core hymns you and your leaders will select as the best embodiment of the Lord's song for your congregation).

Sometimes, those things they already know may not necessarily be the top-drawer material you'll want to nurture as your congregation's staples but will instead be something the laity nevertheless like. I encountered such a situation a couple of years ago at a congregation where I was filling in for a while. They were working on bringing more worship unity among their various services, and the pastor wanted something everyone could sing, regardless of instrumentation, that would serve as a theme song for the last three weeks of the church year. To achieve his aim, we left both the modern song repertoire that predominated at one set of services and the hymnbook that was foremost at another and went with "I'll Fly Away."

Another example comes from almost two decades ago when I picked the old Sunday-school standard "Seek Ye First"[46] as an offertory. Though it was an oldie, I knew it would be familiar to both the folks who favored the music led by our two worship teams as well as to the more traditional crowd. On its own, it would not have made the song list, but with Matthew 6:33 being part of the gospel reading that day, it made perfect sense.

At one of the services, our Schola Cantorum (third- to sixth-grade parish choir) was the choir for the liturgy, so in addition to the other things they sang, I had them add the traditional descant to "Seek Ye First" on the last stanza of the hymn. After the service, a father of one of the choristers came up to me and excitedly told me how much he loved that descant. It turned out he had sung it himself as boy. Even though this hymn was written in the 1960s, a tradition behind it connected the generations. Much joy was discovered.

Similarly, here's testimony of how a perhaps lesser-known hymn has nonetheless strengthened the bond between generations over the years. Many churches have a Hymn of the Day appointed by their denomination that they use alongside a shared lectionary, a set of Scripture readings for each Sunday and holiday. The Hymn of the Day in Lutheran Church—Missouri Synod churches for the Third Sunday in Easter, "With High Delight Let Us Unite,"[47] is not one that jumps off parishioners' lips when they are asked about their favorite Eastertide hymnody. The rhythm can be a bit tricky for singers new to the tune, and many congregations only sing it once a year. As a result, it usually doesn't get the repetition most songs need to work their way into the heart. Yet like "On Jordan's Bank, the Baptist's Cry,"[48] another hymn typically sung once a year, this song has endeared itself to many.

For example, when I was a young cantor in Peoria, Illinois, my children's choir was scheduled to sing the Third Sunday of Easter, so I proceeded to teach them the Hymn of the Day so that they would prepare their own stanza for the Divine Service. Because I was relatively inexperienced and didn't know what the typical self-appointed expert knows about children and song—that kids supposedly don't enjoy hymns and so should be taught ditties and camp songs—I succeeded in having my choristers sing this hymn quite boisterously in short order, and soon their beautiful head tone was projecting nicely across the sanctuary. When Sunday came, one young male chorister was so excited about this hymn that he literally bounced up and down when he sang the third line of the second stanza: "'And yours shall be like victory o'er death and grave,' said he, who gave his life for us, life renewing." (That young man eventually grew up to obtain a doctorate in organ and is now cantor at First Lutheran Church in Boston, leading one of the finest music programs in the Lutheran Church—Missouri Synod.)

Later in the Lord's ministry at that parish, I wrote a trumpet and trombone duet on the tune of "With High Delight" (or "*Mit Freuden Zart*") for a couple of high school kids who, after singing the hymn in choir, were after me the next three years to include it more often so they could play it again. Every time we got together to play, they would smile at me and say, "Cantor! 'With High Delight!' "

The point is that young people, like all of us, like what they know, and if they are taught good stuff, they will like good stuff. Of course, to successfully teach them good stuff, the teacher also has to know and like good stuff. One can't give away something one doesn't have, right? So music teachers need to take substantive yet accessible texts and tunes to heart so that they can in turn inspire the next generation. What will be written on their hearts is up to us. The children do not come into the choir loft or the classroom with a repertoire already in place. They are blank slates. It is up to us to instill in them a love for the best the church has to offer.

As long as we're talking about "With High Delight," I'll share one more story. That same hymn again showed how well good hymns serve the church when a gentleman in my choir, who often traveled on business, went to Germany and attended a congregation of a church body that is in fellowship with my own. This gentleman doesn't speak much German, but he reported that he could still take part because he could follow the liturgy.

This story demonstrates a great benefit of sharing a common liturgy: it unites Christians and allows them to worship together despite language differences. An additional layer of unity, though, was enjoyed by my friend because it happened to be the Third Sunday of Easter when he was there—and the parish he attended sang *"Mit Freuden Zart"*! So he was able not only to say the Apostles' Creed and the Lord's Prayer in English while the congregants spoke in German and to understand the sung parts of the liturgy such as the Gloria, Sanctus, and Agnus Dei, he was also able to sing "With High Delight" along with the congregation. In so doing, he was connected more deeply with his fellow Christians on another continent through the song that we share.

It may seem remarkable that this one, lesser-used hymn has proved in my experience to bring joy in the hearts of children and youth and to strengthen the bonds of unity between Christians who speak different languages. Yet such songs pass from generation to generation and span across the seas, manifesting the unity we have in the Lord. I take such songs to another continent, Africa, in another language, French, and behold the same unity and experience the same joy there. We do well to hold on to songs like this and keep teaching them to our children and proclaiming them throughout all the world.

There is great value in connecting the generations and peoples in this way. Many Lutheran parents are quite moved when the children of the parish sing the Quempas Carol, a longstanding Christmas Eve tradition, especially if the kids are trained and numerous enough to sing in the four corners of the sanctuary, representing the gospel going out to all the world, and to travel from corner to corner between the stanzas as the assembly sings the *Resonet in Laudibus* ("God Himself is born a child, is born a child. God and man are reconciled, are reconciled").

Similarly, many choristers young and old revel in singing the famous David Willcocks descant for "O Come, All Ye Faithful."[49] Our life together in Christ is manifested and celebrated as adults enjoy hearing the next generation sing favorites from their youth and as the youth take hold of what the previous generation has cherished. We are wise to ask how much we miss opportunities to strengthen the ties that bind us when we pick new music. It is so important to stop and ask ourselves what we would sing if we weren't choosing a new piece. We really need to ponder, "Is the new piece really better from the hearer's standpoint? Or is it just something fresh for the director? What is really best for the singers and the hearers?"

These are crucial questions to ask. Churches that don't share the living tradition of the church's song with their children and in their missiology have some more critical questions to ask themselves. What are their kids missing out on? What are the adults missing as well? More importantly, do we really believe the new things we are doing have a good shot at standing the test of time—that they are songs the next generation will want to sing? Or will they quickly fade, thus failing the test of uniting the church's song across the generations? Certainly, there is room for some one-and-done and throwaway music in the life of a congregation, but it should be used intentionally for good reasons—and always in consideration of what would otherwise be done.

This commitment to the big picture—the Lord's song among your people as it is manifested in the living tradition of the repertoire you share as a Christian congregation—keeps the focus on the people's comfort and joy. It's a joy that is for you, too! As one who summons, leads, and nurtures the

Lord's song, you are there with your people in the midst of their praises. You are a catalyst for making this happen. As you do the work of this ministry, you are actually participating in the ongoing, missional work of the Holy Trinity.

Just as Jesus delighted in doing the work of the Father (John 5:17), so you get to participate in the work of the Holy Spirit as he calls, gathers, and enlightens people through the word of God that makes the Father's heart known to them. Inaugurating the heavenly chorus of the eternal song in your corner of the world is part and parcel of the Great Commission. The Spirit is at work through us and in us as God's good and gracious will is unfolded through and in the work of his holy people. And just as Mary rejoiced as she sang the Magnificat (Luke 1:46–55), so, too, do our spirits rejoice as we magnify the Lord and exalt his name together (Ps 34:3).

The joy of the Lord's song is indeed profoundly missional. I've heard Keith Getty more than once call it a "radical witness," and I agree. Steve Martin got a good bit of comedy mileage out of his bluegrass group singing "Atheists Don't Have No Songs," but the sentiment is not just funny, it's true. People sing when they have something to boast about.

There is little joy in existentialism, but there is joy in the Lord. Boasting in our own works is excluded (Rom 3:27), but we rightfully take pride in Christ Jesus, who gives us a song to sing.

And this boast is not something the Lord needs, but it is what the world needs. Mike Salvino, former CEO of Accenture, the world's largest management consulting firm, said, "When people take pride in the business, they focus more on customer needs and deliver innovation."[50] In other words, they are drawn away from themselves and, taking pride in what they are part of, are drawn toward their neighbor.

Similarly, we who have a share in Christ's suffering, death, and resurrection are drawn into his mission when we make the Lord our joy and the topic of our boasting. Scripture teaches repeatedly that our boast should only be in the Lord (Ps 34:2; Jer 9:24; 1 Cor 1:31; Gal 6:14). This has many applications in all areas of congregational life and manifests itself acutely in the church's song.

This comfort and joy are manifest in an attractive way when we make our radical witness to the world, and they are lost when we turn inward and start boasting in our own doing. Just as a company will flounder when it is prouder of its showroom or cutting-edge ad campaign than of the actual goods and services it provides, so, too, does the church miss the mark when we find our joy in the wrong place.

The great twentieth-century theologian Herman Sasse taught much about the "via media," the middle way. He was not talking about compromise but about staying on the right path. Truth is not found between two errors, per se, but there are often ditches of error one can fall into if one veers off either side of the path.

This is certainly true in the worship wars that have resulted in so many congregations losing their common song—and our common boast. On the one hand, we have two generations of new hymnals chock full of excellent hymns and canticles that in many cases are nonetheless forced onto congregations rather than being selectively and convincingly introduced. As wonderful as much of this new music is, few will tell their neighbor, "Come to my church and hear the organ blast songs that few of us know but are really doctrinally pure and liturgically orthodox!"

On the other hand, despite the promises of church-growth gurus and numerous evangelism workshops, the church's experiment with worship styles and adoption of rock bands and radio music over the past thirty years has also not led to boasting in the Lord. As sincere as these missional intentions may be, few congregants are motivated to invite their friends to "come and hear our garage band blast songs that some of us know and sort of sing along with on the easier parts. The songs don't say much, either, but we do them anyway because we're trying to get folks to come."

Ironically, whether one runs off the road to the left or to the right, one is driven by the same motivation: to do things right. The devil's use of our good intentions comes to mind. I don't have all the answers, but I do know they lie in keeping things centered on Christ. So I say this: if you are picking music solely for missional reasons, step back and pick hymns that your people know and love and *can sing* that are about God and his love for us in Christ Jesus. And if you are picking music solely for confessional/orthodox reasons, do the same.

You can test how you are doing by singing a cappella. Take away the wall of sound, whether it is a praise band or an organ, and listen to the people sing. Their singing will reveal to you whether they are boasting in the Lord or not. I was encouraged during my ministry in Oklahoma by the serendipitous power outages we had there. The increasing ability of the congregation to sing without the band helped them understand some of the changes I had introduced into the repertoire as the band had moved from something they worshiped through to a group which instead summoned, empowered, and nurtured them in congregational song.

I am often thankful that the congregations I serve in Africa generally don't have electricity they can count on. While keyboards and guitars, organs and microphones can be great blessings in the right hands, they can also create the illusion of people engaged in a joyful noise. It is best to be able to worship unplugged—just as God's people did in ancient times and just as we did as we "[raised] our Ebenezer"[51] on the American frontier. When the power goes out, the response should not be, "Houston, we have a problem," but "We get to sing a cappella today!"

Cantoral ministry cultivates the common songs that bind the faithful together and moves them to invite others to join in the song. Yes, each generation adds its contributions. Per the motto of the French Reformed Church, "The church is always being reformed," new songs should always be begun. But, remember, people are moved to invite others to church not because the church is singing songs the leaders have decided they should sing but because it is singing the songs their faith wants to sing (Ps 40:3).

CHAPTER 20

Many Will Put Their Trust in the Lord

As I began this book, I pointed out that we find forty-six exhortations and encouragements to sing the Lord's song in Scripture. It bears repeating. Note that these passages are not descriptive but prescriptive. If you include descriptions of singing, the number approaches a hundred. The Lord commands his people to sing, and we respond! He also has attached promises of blessing to those who hear and obey, such as "Many will see and fear, and put their trust in the Lord" (Ps 40:3).

We sing for our own blessing and the blessing of one another, to be sure, but the Lord's song is also a radical witness to the world. No other faith shares a tradition of song like the Christian faith. The gospel has inspired a phenomenon that is unique among world religions; the Holy Spirit breathes into the world a vibrant chorus of joy. The redeemed sing not to earn God's favor but because saving faith cannot keep from singing.

The wise overseer of congregational song trusts the Spirit to do his work through this singing and eschews the world's counsel to divert music toward other goals. This is why we can trust that simple melodies, amateur voices, supportive accompaniment, and even profound silences will accomplish far more than any religious entertainment.

In singing, we pray out loud. Certainly, God hears the meditations of our hearts, but the practice of praying out loud allows one to hear the prayers and thereby be built up in faith as one prays according to the word of God. This blessing also occurs when we sing, but it is extended to those who hear us sing as well. St. Augustine pointed to this when he wrote that "he who sings praise, not only sings, but also loves."[52] What we say and do literally forms us, as our thoughts thus take physical shape in our spoken words, routines, and postures of prayer. What we sing, when we sing, and how we sing forms us in similar, profound ways.

When I visit the sick, I sing. It is primarily for their comfort, but it also makes that radical witness of the joy we have in Christ. In taking requests from those I visit, I am sometimes ministered to as much as the individuals I have come to bless. One such moment, a time when I sang to a total stranger, is seared into my memory. Before patient privacy laws existed as they do now, the congregation I served would be notified of any Missouri Synod Lutherans staying at a nearby hospital. The hospital was a regional one, so we would take on visitation for those from out of town.

On one such visit, I met a dear woman from a town about seventy miles away. I was glad I was able to see her, because it turned out her congregation was in a pastoral vacancy. I came in just a few minutes after the doctors had told her that she had only a week or two left to live. After introductions, conversation, and Scripture, I asked if I might sing for her. She quickly responded with what apparently was one of her favorites. "Oh, sing 'Jesus, Lover of My Soul,' " she said, whereupon I started to look up the words in my hymnal. Then she astonished me, saying, "No, no, don't sing that. That's not what I need to hear right now. I need to hear 'What God Ordains Is Always Good.'"[53] As I

sang all the stanzas to her, she hung attentively on
every word. Looking back, I think I needed that
hymn as much as she did.

What God ordains is always good:
His will is just and holy.
As He directs my life for me,
I follow meek and lowly.
My God indeed in ev'ry need
knows well how He will shield me;
to Him, then, I will yield me.

What God ordains is always good:
He never will deceive me;
He leads me in His righteous way,
and never will He leave me.
I take content what He has sent;
His hand that sends me sadness
will turn my tears to gladness.

What God ordains is always good:
His loving thought attends me;
no poison can be in the cup
that my Physician sends me.
My God is true; each morning new
I trust His grace unending,
My life to Him commending.

What God ordains is always good:
He is my Friend and Father;

He suffers naught to do me harm
though many storms may gather.
Now I may know both joy and woe;
some day I shall see clearly
that He has loved me dearly.

What God ordains is always good:
though I the cup am drinking
which savors now of bitterness,
I take it without shrinking.
For after grief God gives relief,
my heart with comfort filling
and all my sorrow stilling.

What God ordains is always good:
this truth remains unshaken.
Though sorrow, need, or death be mine,
I shall not be forsaken.
I fear no harm, for with His arm
He shall embrace and shield me;
so to my God I yield me.

Faith loves to sing. For several years I noticed a
young man in my former parish come to worship
with his mom. All through his childhood and ado-
lescence he would sing the hymns along with his
mom. Then, as he approached his senior year, he
started mumbling. In college, he stopped singing
altogether. It was heartbreaking.

A couple of years later, one New Year's Eve, he was back, singing joyfully. I can only imagine the reasons, but I suspect it had something to do with the young lady he brought to church with him that evening. Perhaps he was just trying to make a good impression, but people don't sing like that without the joy of the Lord. I know one skates on thin ice when one tries to read motivations into behaviors, so I won't try to diagnose his heart, but such zeal is hard to fake. Whatever his motivation was, I'm glad he found his voice and joined in the Lord's song again. I know the word dwelled in him richly as he did so. May that song stay in his heart and resound on his lips all the days of his life.

I am not saying that singing is an absolute measure of faith. Some have more skill than others, experience varies, cultures are different, medical issues arise. Some, sadly, were told they can't sing when they were young and live with the scars. But I do believe faith wants to sing. Faith is living and active and full of joy. Luther even went so far as to say,

> God has made our hearts and spirits cheerful through his dear Son, whom he has given us to redeem us from sin, death,

and the devil. Whoever truly believes this cannot help it—he must sing and speak of it with good cheer and joy, so that others also hear of it and come to it. But whoever does not want to sing and speak of it? That's a sign that he doesn't believe it and is not in the new and cheerful covenant, but instead he still belongs under the old, lazy, and miserable covenant.[54]

One might paraphrase that simply as "those who will not sing show thereby a lack of faith," or, as we sing in the gospel hymn "Marching to Zion":[55]

> Let those refuse to sing who never knew
>   our God;
> But children of the heavenly King may
>   speak their joys abroad.

It's true. Particularly among those who aren't musicians. There are those who honor God with their lips whose hearts are far from him, to be sure (Matt 15:8; Isa 29:13), and one finds people who are involved in church for the music rather than singing the Lord's song because of Jesus, so one must take care and never judge.

But there is a consequence to saving faith. God changes people in Christ by the Holy Spirit, and it is a change that can be heard. Not in the quantity or the beauty of sound but in the joy. I think that is easiest to perceive in the non-musician, so I have found the greatest satisfaction in my work over the years not in beautiful choral performances I have conducted (of which I do have fond memories and for which I am thankful) but when I see and hear these folks singing the liturgy and the hymns. I just love it!

There are so many joys I could share, such as the eighth-grade boy who changed from his family's non-singing habits and started joining in. His hymnal was open for every hymn, including the Communion hymns. He would sit up straight and sing every stanza. Over time, it seemed to have an effect on his parents, who began to at least open their hymnals and follow along. Sometimes the radical witness of the Lord's song is needed by the person in the pew in front of you or even the family member next to you.

Or seeing acolytes sing. I don't usually see this when I visit other congregations. Most acolyte programs don't develop a singing culture, and often the acolytes are drafted from the confirmation class.

The congregations I've served long-term have had volunteer acolyte programs, which helps in many ways, and in those places, I've worked with the ministry team to advance a singing culture.

Still, adolescents are particularly shy when they are in front of hundreds of people. Yet several times, pastors sitting alongside them have noted how much they have enjoyed the acolytes' singing. While not all of them sing out, they can and will do so when true congregational song becomes the norm. They will sing "Salvation Unto Us Has Come"[56] just as they sing "Happy Birthday."

It really is great to hear faith singing. In 1994, on vacation in Nebraska, I went a bit out of my way to hear a well-known organist on Sunday morning at his congregation in Omaha. I sat in the pew in front of a mother accompanied by two young-adult daughters. It was great singing with these ladies, who sang the liturgy robustly behind me with obviously untrained yet sincere voices. My chat with them afterwards confirmed that they had no formal musical training. They chuckled when I complimented them and suggested they join the choir. They did not consider themselves at all to be candidates. No, they simply sang the Lord's song, without shyness or hesitation, because of the faith the Lord had given them—and because that famous organist turned out also to be a true Lutheran cantor. He paid utmost attention to leading the people in the church's song, and the congregation in turn embraced their participation in worship. They understood that the Lord's song was not something for professionals or for fellow members with some mysterious gift. They sang out because they knew that singing the Lord's song was simply what Christians do.

Yes, faith sings. Isn't it great to hear it?

CHAPTER 21

Be Prepared

In what I have shared in this book, I hope I have communicated what a joy and privilege it is to serve the Lord by leading his people in song. I am blessed to have been able to do this work for so many years.

Still, it is not for the faint of heart. One must be of good courage to undertake this course. The devil, the world, and our sinful natures wage strong attacks against those who sing the Lord's song—particularly against those who dare to lead and encourage it. One can, and must, preach Christ, but congregants will readily tune out the preacher, if they are paying attention at all, and grab whatever kernels from the sermon they find agreeable. One can, and must, teach Christ, but many regular churchgoers avoid Bible studies or select alternative studies that please man's itching ears.

But if the service sings Christ, watch out: many will loudly object. And one may be surprised at who joyfully accepts this path and who rebels against it. The word of God is always a two-edged sword, and singing the word has proven to be a particularly sharp one. Less resistance will come if you shy away from this "third rail" of ministry, but the path of least resistance may lead away from Christ rather than toward him.

If, as I hope, this reading has motivated you to engage in worship renewal in your congregation, here is some advice. You may think that your ministry has led people to this point—that perhaps after having been taught and preached the word, they are ready to really sing it. But, for many Christians, making any claims for worship at all is an offense. Whether they smell Romanism or ritualism or Pentecostalism or whatever-*ism*, they know that any teaching comes with truth claims, and they resist any claims about worship lest such call into question any of their feelings or preferences.

So even some who agree with your preaching and teaching will side with those who push back and say, "Let's just praise the Lord." Sadly, this attitude denies them the power and comfort that the Lord delivers through the word dwelling in them richly, but it is an understandable concern, which you need to be prepared to address patiently, confidently, and lovingly.

I have experienced this myself. In a previous parish, although there was overall a very positive reaction to the things the ministry team was doing to nourish the Lord's song there, people took issue with the teaching about worship. Ironically, the very thing that was supposed to help people understand the changes and make them go better actually proved to be what some people found provocative!

It took me years to figure out why this was so, but I think I have a handle on it now: some think liturgy is only for the sake of good order and that what goes on in the service is just making an offering to God, so *teaching about worship offends them because it makes other claims.* They react viscerally because they don't understand God's role in worship and conclude that the pastor and musician are puffed up, viewing what they do more highly than they ought. As a result, they perceive any changes in practice or elevation of new music as inherent criticism of whatever was done before—which they take as judging their dear brothers and sisters.

Of course, sometimes it is necessary to say that what was done before was not proper, right, and salutary. But if care is taken to affirm one's predecessors and proceed with humility, most people can be led to understand that exercising good judgment does not mean judging people. For those who are unable to come to that understanding, it is important not to let their attitudes hold back the church. Excellence and success are the best persuasion. If necessary, explanations can wait.

Still, when resistance is significant, it may be necessary to slow down. I recall one prominent elder who objected to sung prayer cadences, which are commonplace in the Lutheran tradition. He pointed to Jesus' admonition against "vain repetitions" (Matt 6:7 KJV) and argued that people weren't praying by singing "Lord, have mercy" but were instead being conditioned to respond in a mindless way. His position was that the truly pious practice was for everyone to listen to the pastor pray at length and then, if they wished, to whisper a quiet "Amen."

I attempted to show him from Scripture that Jesus' words against "vain repetitions" referred to

the babbling of those who thought that their efforts
to repeat God-pleasing words were somehow meritorious before God. I agreed that the context of
this passage would seem to include the showy
practices of the hypocrites in the synagogue, but
he would not agree that the problem was the vanity
of an ungodly heart rather than the repetition of
a sung refrain.

One could fairly argue we should have dis-
continued the practice for the sake of the weaker
brother (1 Cor 8:11), as sometimes one best forgoes
good for the sake of the weak. However, allowing
individuals to veto the deliberations of the congregation is unhealthy for the body of Christ and
invites questions about other's weaknesses—to wit,
who is the weaker brother? What if the weaker
brother needs to submit to a further weaker
brother?

Ultimately, the discussion must return to Jesus.
While one must honor all the stakeholders in the
church, we must also be on guard against worshiping according to rules made by men (Matt
15:9). Sometimes, if someone in power binds consciences by establishing rules that God has not
given, one makes the good confession by exercising
freedom for the sake of the gospel. So, discernment

is required. Can an accommodation be made that does not compromise the gospel? Is this something about which we can disagree without binding consequences, pressing on together in spite of our differences and trusting that our unity in Christ will prevail (Phil 3:12–16)?

As my dear mentor in ministry, the sainted Rev. Gerald Freudenburg, once told me, "You have to have a thick skin in music ministry, Phil. Everyone has opinions about church music, and few are hesitant to share them."

Such is especially true today, when some have the idea that the church musician's opinions on worship should be disregarded for the very reason that he or she has special training and skills that get in the way of relating to the average churchgoer. Through the years, I've known hostile voices at voters' assemblies, dealt with agitated elders, and missed time with family so that I could patiently listen to parishioner complaints. It comes with the territory.

Even as you keep striving toward the ultimate goal of vibrant singing of holy song, you will need to be patient and charitable. Remember that retreat is not surrender but a time-honored strategy. Sometimes you need to regroup. In doing so you can avoid casualties and even gain allies. In a former parish, I had two allies who really got behind me after I agreed not to use the tune *Austria* anymore. It is a fine tune, written by a classical composer (Haydn), and so I was pleased to program it one Sunday, as the text we had with it in our hymnal fit right in with the pastor's sermon theme. It is not unfamiliar and is quite singable, and the congregation did very well with it. Unfortunately, that tune was sullied during WWII. Instead of "Glorious Things of You Are Spoken,"[57] two members—a Jewish convert and a lady who lived through the war as a child in Germany—heard "*Deutschland, Deutschland über alles.*" The mind works by association and so this tune was a stumbling block for them. They were most appreciative that I assured them I would not use it again.

A similar event occurred more recently when it turned out I programmed a piece for a children's choir that just happened to use a tune that brought back very bad memories for a parent. The mom was nice enough to say it was okay to use it, but I told her there was plenty of other music we could sing. The point is: *you don't have to be right.* Yes, there are times for the sake of the gospel where it is necessary not to bind consciences, but Galatians 6:2 must prevail: "Bear one another's burdens, and so fulfill the law of Christ." If you are being opposed by those who would dampen the gospel, then stand firm. But don't let that be an excuse for your pride, your preferences, or your will if by relenting you can be "all things to all people" (1 Cor 9:22) and bring a weaker soul closer to Jesus. It's just the right thing to do, and it is also the wise thing to do. I've found that those weaker souls often become your strongest allies after they have experienced your love for them.

Such bending for the sake of others may mean the quality of music suffers a bit here and there. Which is fine. Remember, if you are seeking applause, music ministry—at least, faithful music ministry—is not for you. There are places you can play and sing and provide whatever ears want to hear—whether the latest sounds from Nashville in one place or classical sacred music concerts in another. Even where applause during the service might not be the tradition, one can find churches that primarily use music to seek the approval of man. But such falls short of the high and holy calling of the church musician to lead God's people in singing his song.

The one who pursues caring for souls through the art of music will face some tough decisions. Sometimes it will be necessary to bend for the weaker brother, other times to find the courage and strength to press on. Sometimes it will be time to admit you are wrong and, if you have caused offense, to ask for forgiveness. Moses and Elijah, who both knew the joys, challenges, disappointments, and fatigue that accompany the Lord's ministry, can help here. One of the best questions to ask when one is facing those tough times in music ministry is, "Am I choosing music Moses and Elijah would like to sing?"

The answer is not something you need to speculate about. Luke's account of the Transfiguration provides it for you. When Moses and Elijah appeared on the mountain with Jesus, the Scripture says they were speaking about his *exodus* or *departure*, "which he was about to accomplish at Jerusalem" (Luke 9:31). Transported from the heavenly throne, where the redeemed sing of the triumph of the Lamb (Rev 15:2–4), they were still taking part in the eternal libretto about God's saving acts, from his foreshadowing of the redemption of humanity through the deliverance of his people through the Red Sea to the ultimate salvation delivered by his blood on the cross. If that's what you are singing about, don't let a weaker brother or sister muffle your voice. For Jerusalem's sake, you cannot keep quiet (Isa 62:1).

So, bend and slow down, as needed, out of patience and love, but press on nonetheless, knowing that the Lord is with you. Trust that those whom the Spirit is calling, gathering, enlightening, and sanctifying among you will be persuaded in the end. Let it happen, and while you can and should teach along the way, know also that some things are better caught than taught, and many learn better by doing.

As eloquent as you may be, sometimes words get in the way—especially when it comes to music. As the great jazz pianist Thelonious Monk said, "Talking about music is like dancing about architecture."[58] So, instead of trying to win the argument, earn people's trust and let God do the convincing through psalms, hymns, and spiritual songs. After all, his thoughts are higher than your thoughts (Isa 55:9).

Above all, don't embark on this journey alone. Pastors and cantors need to be in a relationship similar to a good marriage, with the pastor loving his musician like Christ loves the church and the chief musician loving his pastor as the church adores its Lord (Eph 5).

This means, pastors, that you should not hide decisions from the cantor, manipulate her, or treat him like a child. It also means you don't get to simply hand over all "worship stuff" to your partner in ministry and pat yourself on the back for being a good delegator. The musician serves a vital role in the ministry which you oversee, and you are called to invest in it, understand it, and support it. You don't do that by checking the box by hiring the right staff person. Above all, united in the Lord's ministry with your cantor, you are to be his or her champion/advocate, just as a good husband always speaks well of his wife, defends her, and zealously guards her reputation. Be ready to lay down your life for her.

Similarly, musicians, you are always to speak well of the pastor. Many will come to you with complaints about him. Do not share in their gossip. Put the best construction on everything he does, and submit to his leadership just as the church submits to Christ.

This doesn't mean you never complain, but like a good wife talks to her husband and doesn't argue in front of the children, you keep your disagreements private. Take care not to show any displeasure in front of the congregation, especially on Sunday morning. Show your love not just by what you say or don't say but also in what you do. Listen attentively to the pastor's preaching and be respectful of all that is done in the service, even if you are not in front of the congregation but out of sight in the back of the worship space or in a balcony. You are to assist the pastor in the care of souls. Your care for them is seriously compromised when there is division between you. Even when disagreement persists, take care not to show it.

I should add that if a problem between the pastor and the musician is not a professional disagreement but actual sin, it needs to be confessed and forgiven. If repentance is lacking, then involve others as appropriate, according to how your church follows Matthew 18:15–20. Private outside counsel can also be helpful. With appropriate discretion, pastors and cantors may seek the advice of ecclesiastical supervisors, professional counselors, and, of course, spouses and parents. This is wholly consistent with Christian love.

Church politics necessarily come into play in all of this. I am using the word "politics" here not as a pejorative but in its pure sense of governance.

Whether a congregation is getting along or is in conflict, there are a congregational power structure, pastoral leadership styles, boards and committees, and congregational culture and history to navigate. All of these are formed of many interesting and complex personalities that are as unpredictable as Forrest Gump's proverbial box of chocolates.

For navigating the complexities of church politics when considering a change in practice, here are some questions I have found helpful to ask. Along with asking these questions, always be careful to first imagine a world where the desired innovation never existed and then consider whether the innovation is truly best or whether something else might be better.

First ask, does the innovation only affect you, or does it affect the pastor, other staff, or the whole assembly? People are more accepting of change when it only affects others. They tend to be more resistant if the change would affect their own pattern of worship.

Next ask, does the innovation overtly serve the text, or is it more subtle? When people are surprised by something obvious, they more readily get it and embrace it. If it is more subtle, though, they may need some teaching. Otherwise it may appear that you are promoting change merely for the sake of change.

Finally, you should ask, will the innovation be done well? This question may seem obvious, but sometimes it is not. For example, if you are going to use percussion for the first time, it is important to make sure it is done well. Otherwise, you risk people reacting negatively to the poor execution.

Similarly, be sure the people will hear excellence the first time the children's choir chants a part of the liturgy or the first time handbells play a free ring on a doxological stanza. Ideally, these things would always be well done. However, I've too often witnessed good ideas that were poorly implemented, resulting in a lost opportunity. People don't respond well to what is poorly planned or executed, and the opportunity to enrich liturgical life ends up being squandered.

So, to follow up on the examples above: if you are going to have the children do something radically new in the service, make sure they have memorized their part and understand precisely where it fits in. At your rehearsal, prepare them with whatever precedes it so they are prepared to go with the flow. As for the handbells, make sure the musicians know exactly how you are going to get them in and out of that free ring, particularly how they are to dampen their bells at the end. There are so many things that wind up not going well not because the musicians didn't know their part but because sufficient time was not spent making sure they would flow well in the actual service. It is the leader, not those serving, who bears the responsibility when this happens.

Thinking through the who, what, where, when, and how of what we do reminds us that failing to make decisions still results in making a choice. However much this book may have persuaded or inspired you to be more attentive to the Lord's song, remember that the song will go on regardless. Failure to plan is still a plan. In other words, if you choose not to confront decisions about worship, you are still making a choice.

These questions remain: Will you sing of the works of the Lord? Will you engage your people and encourage them to lift up their hearts? Will you play humbly and skillfully? Will you be who you are and sing what you can sing? Will you use the precious time, talents, and opportunities the Lord has given you to grow a singing culture? Will you invite them to join the chorus of faith? Those with temporal power over us may no longer demand from us a song, as the Israelites' captors demanded of them (see Ps 137:3), but they still need to hear it, and so do we.

It is a daunting challenge, but take heart: the Lord will give you all you need as you place your trust in him. With the Lord at your side, you've got what it takes! Remember, this is his ministry, not yours. And he takes care of his church.

If you rely solely on your own musicianship to somehow win over the folks, you will fail. The same is true if you think the winsomeness of your personality will convince objectors. You should always be kind and speak the truth in love, but if the case is to be made on the basis of your expertise or skill, you will fail to convince. This is especially true in this age of great subjectivity, where the arts are viewed as expressions of personality, feelings, and emotions.

But with the Lord all things are possible. Ground yourself personally in the Lord through daily repentance, prayer, and meditation on the word, and ground your music in the expression of the same. There you will have the inexhaustible resources you will need to uphold your spirit and lead your people into singing for joy.

So with the psalmist we say, "Oh sing to the LORD a new song; sing to the LORD, all the earth! Sing to the LORD, bless his name; tell of his salvation from day to day" (Ps 96:1–2).

Where to Begin

Some churches conclude worship with what's called a "postlude." It follows the benediction, as people are leaving the service. Sometimes, if the music grabs people's attention, a good number of them will stay and listen. Usually, though, they exit during the postlude. That's fine: a postlude's purpose, after all, is to accompany the people's departure, reinforcing what they have just heard as they leave the house of God filled with the Holy Spirit.

This postlude is a bit different. Rather than amplifying a mood, this accompaniment is for the reader who, having considered the thoughts herein, may be inspired to embark on a path of worship renewal but is not sure where to begin. Perhaps you want to sing more classic hymns but don't know the repertoire. Or perhaps you have a congregation that is unfamiliar with the church's treasury of song but are not sure how to go about nurturing a core set of hymns. Or you have a set of modern songs you wish your people to really take to heart but want some ideas as to how to organize them. So here are some thoughts about how to cultivate a core hymnody in your congregation, so that you may have an example of how the ideas of this book may be put to use.

As HAS BEEN DISCUSSED EARLIER, THE PSALMS are the Bible's hymnal, and God clearly intends for us to sing them. I would like to begin, therefore, by suggesting a couple of resources for doing so. How one goes about singing the psalms depends on a congregation's musical resources and the singing tradition of its people. Some congregations will enjoy singing psalms in many styles; others will prefer the consistency of one or two.

Two resources provide multiple excellent options for singing every psalm, and I highly recommend getting them: *Psalms for All Seasons* (Brazos Press, 2012) and *Christian Worship: Psalter* (Northwest Publishing House, 2021). If you are a pastor or lay leader, get these for your chief musician; if you are a musician, get them for yourself. Once you find the right singing styles for your congregation, these resources will lead you to more settings in those particular styles. Some of the possibilities include simple formulas for chanting the psalm, hymn paraphrases, psalms with through-composed[59] verses for the leader and refrains for the assembly, contemporary song settings, and choruses from the Taizé community. Enjoy trying out the various styles. You will be surprised at what you discover. Singing God's word has a way of revealing things.

As for hymns, I recommend following a five-year plan that provides for the introduction or reintroduction of a set of sixty core hymns at a pace of one per month (a "hymn of the month"). Hymns or songs that are totally unfamiliar should first be lined out for the congregation. This involves having a capable singer who knows the hymn sing each line of the first stanza of the hymn one line at a time, with the people repeating back what they have heard. It's important that the one who is teaching is able to do so from memory so that he or she can maintain eye contact and fully engage with the assembly. The leader should not sing when the people do. This allows him or her to listen, receive, and affirm the singing and to know whether that line needs another effort or the group can move on to the next line. At the end of the process, the whole stanza should be sung, beginning to end. This step can be skipped if the core hymn is already somewhat known and is merely being reviewed or reintroduced. As these hymns of the month are learned, they should continue to be sung at least four times a year so that they stay in the congregation's collective heart.

During the month in which a hymn or song is featured—particularly if it is being introduced for the first time—it should not merely be sung four weeks in a row but truly *featured*. Instrumentalists should play compositions or improvise on the tunes during the attendant music (prelude, offering collection, Communion distribution, postlude) throughout the month. During the first service at which the hymn is introduced, all the attendant music should ideally feature the tune; in subsequent weeks, at least one of the three or four slots should do so. The tune should also be presented in a variety of ways, with different instruments and in different styles. Additionally, the choir(s) and soloists in the congregation should learn the hymn so that they can adorn its singing with choral or solo stanzas or descants (or, at the very least, fortify the congregation as it learns the hymn). Obviously, this will call for a good deal of advanced planning on the part of the worship leaders!

For a hymn of the month that is already in the congregation's song list, it may be sufficient to give a special arrangement of the hymn to a soloist one of the four weeks. But whatever you do, be creative. Seek to sustain interest. And, perhaps most important, educate. Congregational publications should promote each month's hymn by explaining its scriptural and doctrinal content, teaching about the author of the text and composer of the tune, and directing people to where they might hear quality vocal and instrumental music on the hymn. Today these are often readily and freely available on music streaming platforms.

To HELP YOU GET STARTED ON YOUR OWN CORE hymnody journey, I offer below a sample list with two sets of hymns: thirty ecumenical hymns held by a good number of Christian traditions, and thirty appropriate for a Lutheran congregation. I present these two sets for two reasons: first, to demonstrate how a congregation can sing a mix of hymns held in common with other Christians while also nurturing a good mix that upholds its own tradition and reinforces its doctrinal distinctives, and second, to show how one can do this using a denominational hymnal, as most hymnals today include such a mix. So the presence of my denomination's *Lutheran Service Book* (*LSB*) is not just practical in that I used it as a chief reference throughout this book, but this list drawn from it demonstrates a hymnody that includes denominational distinctives while embracing the song of the broader church.

Of course, any attempt to embrace the broader church has limitations. A core hymnody can reflect the universality of the church, but it cannot fully represent it. So you will notice that I have only included a couple of global hymns: a hymn from Latin America of Presbyterian origin ("Holy Spirit, the Dove Sent from Heaven") and a hymn from Lutherans in Tanzania ("Christ Has Arisen, Alleluia!"). These have both proven very popular where they have been sung in North America, and they have excellent tunes and texts. So catholicity is acknowledged in these lists via the inclusion of a couple of hymns from the Global South and a Roman Catholic hymn for Maundy Thursday

("When You Woke that Thursday Morning"). In addition, the hymns in both groups were curated to balance ancient, Reformation, Colonial-era, and modern tunes and texts. Such a balance is a reminder that the song of the church—and the great cloud of witnesses—transcends boundaries not only of place but of time.

Another consideration in the compiling of this list was a conscious effort to exclude songs that have broad familiarity beyond congregational song. So, for example, standard Christmas carols are omitted, as well as hymns such as "Amazing Grace" and "Jesus Loves Me." You can certainly put such hymns on your list if you think they merit cultivation, but my sample list presupposes a certain amount of enduring legacy. At the same time, even a congregation that knows well a hymn such as "O Come, O Come, Emmanuel" might benefit from marinating in it for an Advent season. Ultimately, you should trust your instincts and adapt accordingly.

Readers who wish to adapt the second set of the list below to conform to their ministry needs should note that some hymns generally considered to be ecumenical are from the Lutheran tradition and so were put on that second list. Thus, you might either want to keep these in your own second set or move hymns such as "Now Thank We All Our God," "A Mighty Fortress," and "O Sacred Head, Now Wounded" to your ecumenical list. Here again, trust your judgment.

Finally, you may note that my favorite feast day, the Transfiguration of Our Lord, is included among the hymns for the church year. It has become a significant holy day in some circles, but I know many churches do not observe it, so you can certainly replace it with something else if you wish. My suggestion would be one I just barely left off my list, the hymn paraphrase of the ancient hymn of praise, the Te Deum: "Holy God, We Praise Thy Name" (*LSB* 940). It has global appeal—and could even be a good choice for starting off the series.

IF YOU CHOOSE TO EMBARK ON A CORE hymnody or hymn renewal plan, you should, above all, fully flesh out the plan before you begin and do so in conjunction with the other members of your ministry team. Be transparent with the congregation, and let your passion for the project persuade those who may need some winsome convincing. You may need to tweak the plan, but such tweaking should be minimal and done in view of the whole project. Don't improvise as you go along. If a powerful idea does come along, delay the plan a month in order to capture the moment but then circle back to your plan. Publish the plan so that you are transparent with your people and so that you and your team can better stay on point.

When it is integrated into the life of the church through choir rehearsals, Sunday school, church newsletters, the church website, and, yes, the pastor's sermons, a hymn renewal project such as this will yield great benefit toward the making of disciples. As your people sing the story of God's love, they will indeed observe the just decrees of the Lord and take to heart his holy word.

Thirty Ecumenical Core Hymns for English-Speaking North Americans

1. Advent: "Come, Thou Long-Expected Jesus" (LSB 338)

2. Christmas: "Of the Father's Love Begotten" (LSB 384)

3. Christmas: "Once in Royal David's City" (LSB 376)

4. Epiphany: "Brightest and Best of the Stars of the Morning" (LSB 400)

5. Transfiguration: "O Wondrous Type! O Vision Fair!" (LSB 413)

6. Lent: "My Song Is Love Unknown" (LSB 430)

7. Lent: "When I Survey the Wondrous Cross" (LSB 425, 426)

8. Palm Sunday: "All Glory, Laud, and Honor" (LSB 442)

9. Maundy Thursday: "When You Woke That Thursday Morning" (LSB 445)

10. Good Friday: "Stricken, Smitten, and Afflicted" (LSB 451)

11. Easter: "Jesus Christ Is Risen Today" (LSB 457)

12. Eastertide: "The Day of Resurrection" (LSB 478)

13. Ascension: "A Hymn of Glory Let Us Sing" (LSB 493)

14. Pentecost: "Holy Spirit, the Dove Sent from Heaven" (LSB 502)

15. Holy Trinity: "Holy, Holy, Holy" (LSB 504)

16. Justification: "My Hope Is Built on Nothing Less" (LSB 576)

17. Sanctification: "Love Divine, All Loves Excelling" (LSB 700)

18. Baptism: "We Know that Christ Is Raised" (LSB 603)

19. Communion: "Draw Near and Take the Body of the Lord" (LSB 637)

20. Morning: "Awake, My Soul, and with the Sun" (LSB 868)

21. Evening: "Abide with Me" (LSB 878).

22. Death and Burial: "I Know That My Redeemer Lives" (LSB 461)

23. Church Militant: "Come, We That Love the Lord" ("Marching to Zion") (LSB 669)

24. Church Triumphant: "For All the Saints" (LSB 677)

25. Fellowship of Believers: "The Church's One Foundation" (LSB 644)

26. Trust: "The King of Love, My Shepherd Is" (LSB 709)

27. Cross and Comfort: "Be Still, My Soul" (LSB 752)

28. Mission and Witness: "Hark, the Voice of Jesus Crying" (LSB 826)

29. Thanksgiving: "For the Fruits of His Creation" (LSB 894)

30. Thanksgiving: "Come, You Thankful People, Come" (LSB 892)

THIRTY LUTHERAN CORE
HYMNS FOR ENGLISH-SPEAKING
NORTH AMERICANS*

1. Advent: "O Lord, How Shall I Meet You" (LSB 334)

2. Advent: "Savior of the Nations, Come" (LSB 332)

3. Christmas: "Let All Together Praise Our God" (LSB 389)

4. Epiphany: "O Morning Star, How Fair and Bright" (LSB 395)

5. Transfiguration: "'Tis Good Lord, to Be Here" (LSB 414)

6. Lent: "Christ the Life of All the Living" (LSB 420)

7. Lent: "Sing, My Tongue, the Glorious Battle" (LSB 454)

8. Passion Sunday: "A Lamb Goes Uncomplaining Forth" (LSB 438)

9. Maundy Thursday: "O Lord, We Praise Thee" (LSB 617)

10. Good Friday: "O Sacred Head, Now Wounded" (LSB 450)

11. Easter: "Awake, My Heart with Gladness" (LSB 467)

12. Eastertide: "Christ Has Arisen, Alleluia" (LSB 466)

13. Ascension: "Up Through Endless Ranks of Angels" (LSB 491)

14. Pentecost: "Come, Holy Ghost, God and Lord" (LSB 497)

15. Holy Trinity: "O God, O Lord of Heaven and Earth" (LSB 834)

16. Justification: "Salvation unto Us Has Come" (LSB 555)

17. Sanctification: "Jesus, Thy Boundless Love to Me" (LSB 683)

18. The Church: "Built on the Rock" (LSB 645)

19. Morning: "With the Lord Begin Your Task" (LSB 869)

20. Evening: "Now Rest Beneath Night's Shadow" (LSB 880)

21. Death and Burial: "Oh, How Blest Are They" (LSB 679)

22. Church Triumphant: "Behold a Host, Arrayed in White" (LSB 676)

23. Reformation: "Lord, Keep Us Steadfast in Your Word" (LSB 655)

24. Holy Baptism: "God's Own Child, I Gladly Say It" (LSB 594)

25. Holy Communion: "Soul, Adorn Thyself with Gladness" (LSB 636)

26. Trust: "Lord, Thee I Love with All My Heart" (LSB 708)

27. Fellowship of Believers: "Where Charity and Love Prevail" (LSB 845)

28. Cross and Comfort: "What God Ordains Is Always Good" (LSB 760)

29. Mission and Witness: "O Christ Our True and Only Light" (LSB 839)

30. Thanksgiving: "Now Thank We All Our God" (LSB 895)

* Adapt and/or replace according to theological and cultural tradition (see above).

Acknowledgments

I WOULD LIKE TO GIVE THANKS FOR THE FOL-
lowing people, each of whom have made this work
possible in their own unique ways:

Rev. Dr. Hal Senkbeil, for his profound understanding of the role of music in spiritual care, his
professional support over two decades, and his
encouragement to write this book.

My wife, Cheryl Magness, to whom this book
is dedicated, for helping me carve out time to write
and then expertly editing my first drafts.

My dear children, Trevor, Caitlin, and Evan, for
always supporting and championing their father in
his vocation, even when it meant making sacrifices.

Rev. Ralph Hobratschk, who called a struggling,
twenty-something jazz musician and told him he
was needed in the choir loft.

My spiritual father in the faith, Rev. Gerald V.
Freudenburg (1933–2010), who lovingly mentored

me in ministry and formed a cantor out of a music teacher.

Dr. Charles Brown, who taught me how to listen to the human spirits behind the voices I conduct and made me a better leader of whole congregations in the process.

Rev. John Wilke, for keeping my eyes turned upon Jesus during hard times.

Nathan Beethe, Stephen R. Johnson, and Miguel Ruiz, fellow Lutheran cantors and dear friends, for their spiritual counsel and professional wisdom.

Rev. Dr. James Marriott, for giving me use of his home during his family vacation so that I had a quiet place to write many chapters.

The children in all my children's choirs over the years, for keeping me energized and reminding me each week why Jesus upheld the faith of children as a model for us.

APPENDIX

The Lord's Song
Bible Passages

SCRIPTURAL EXHORTATIONS AND ENCOURAGE-
MENTS to sing the Lord's song:

Deuteronomy 31:19—"Now therefore write this
song and teach it to the people of Israel. Put it in
their mouths, that this song may be a witness for
me against the people of Israel."

1 Chronicles 16:9—"Sing to him, sing praises to
him; tell of all his wondrous works!"

1 Chronicles 16:23—"Sing to the LORD, all the
earth! Tell of his salvation from day to day."

2 Chronicles 20:21—"And when he had taken counsel with the people, he appointed those who were
to sing to the LORD and praise him in holy attire, as

they went before the army, and say, 'Give thanks to the LORD, for his steadfast love endures forever.' "

Psalm 5:11—"But let all who take refuge in you rejoice; let them ever sing for joy, and spread your protection over them, that those who love your name may exult in you."

Psalm 9:11—"Sing praises to the LORD, who sits enthroned in Zion! Tell among the peoples his deeds!"

Psalm 30:4—"Sing praises to the LORD, O you his saints, and give thanks to his holy name."

Psalm 33:3—"Sing to him a new song; play skillfully on the strings, with loud shouts."

Psalm 47:1—"Clap your hands, all peoples! Shout to God with loud songs of joy!"

Psalm 47:6–7—"Sing praises to God, sing praises! Sing praises to our King, sing praises! For God is King of all the earth; sing praises with a psalm!"

Psalm 66:2—"Sing the glory of his name; give to him glorious praise!"

Psalm 67:4—"Let the nations be glad and sing for joy, for you judge the peoples with equity and guide the nations upon earth. *Selah.*"

Psalm 68:4—"Sing to God, sing praises to his name; lift up a song to him who rides through the deserts; his name is the LORD; exult before him!"

Psalm 68:32—"O kingdoms of the earth, sing to God; sing praises to the Lord, *Selah.*"

Psalm 81:1—"Sing aloud to God our strength; shout for joy to the God of Jacob!"

Psalm 81:2—"Raise a song; sound the tambourine, the sweet lyre with the harp."

Psalm 96:1-2—"Oh sing to the LORD a new song; sing to the LORD, all the earth! Sing to the LORD, bless his name; tell of his salvation from day to day."

Psalm 98:1—"Oh sing to the LORD a new song, for he has done marvelous things! His right hand and his holy arm have worked salvation for him."

Psalm 98:4-5—Make a joyful noise to the LORD, all the earth; break forth into joyous song and sing praises! Sing praises to the LORD with the lyre, with the lyre and the sound of melody!"

Psalm 100:2—"Serve the LORD with gladness! Come into his presence with singing!"

Psalm 105:2—"Sing to him, sing praises to him; tell of all his wondrous works!"

Psalm 107:22—"And let them offer sacrifices of thanksgiving, and tell of his deeds in songs of joy!"

Psalm 135:3—"Praise the LORD, for the LORD is good; sing to his name, for it is pleasant!"

Psalm 147:1—"Praise the LORD! For it is good to sing praises to our God; for it is pleasant, and a song of praise is fitting."

Psalm 147:7—"Sing to the LORD with thanksgiving; make melody to our God on the lyre!"

Psalm 149:1—"Praise the LORD! Sing to the LORD a new song, his praise in the assembly of the godly!"

Psalm 149:5—"Let the godly exult in glory; let them sing for joy on their beds."

Isaiah 12:5–6—"Sing praises to the LORD, for he has done gloriously; let this be made known in all the earth. Shout, and sing for joy, O inhabitant of Zion, for great in your midst is the Holy One of Israel."

Isaiah 23:16—"Take a harp; go about the city, O forgotten prostitute! Make sweet melody; sing many songs, that you may be remembered."

Isaiah 26:19—"Your dead shall live; their bodies shall rise. You who dwell in the dust, awake and sing for joy! For your dew is a dew of light, and the earth will give birth to the dead."

Isaiah 42:10—"Sing to the LORD a new song, his praise from the end of the earth, you who go down to the sea, and all that fills it, the coastlands and their inhabitants."

Isaiah 42:11—"Let the desert and its cities lift up their voice, the villages that Kedar inhabits; let the habitants of Sela sing for joy, let them shout from the top of the mountains."

Isaiah 44:23—"Sing, O heavens, for the LORD has done it; shout, O depths of the earth; break forth into singing, O mountains, O forest, and every tree in it! For the LORD has redeemed Jacob, and will be glorified in Israel."

Isaiah 49:13—"Sing for joy, O heavens, and exult, O earth; break forth, O mountains, into singing!

For the LORD has comforted his people and will have compassion on his afflicted."

Isaiah 52:9—"Break forth together into singing, you waste places of Jerusalem, for the LORD has comforted his people; he has redeemed Jerusalem."

Isaiah 54:1—"'Sing, O barren one, who did not bear; break forth into singing and cry aloud, you who have not been in labor! For the children of the desolate one will be more than the children of her who is married,' says the LORD."

Jeremiah 20:13—"Sing to the LORD; praise the LORD! For he has delivered the life of the needy from the hand of evildoers."

Jeremiah 31:7—"For thus says the LORD: 'Sing aloud with gladness for Jacob, and raise shouts for the chief of the nations; proclaim, give praise, and say, "O LORD, save your people, the remnant of Israel." ' "

Zephaniah 3:14—"Sing aloud, O daughter of Zion; shout, O Israel! Rejoice and exult with all your heart, O daughter of Jerusalem!"

Zechariah 2:10—"Sing and rejoice, O daughter of Zion, for behold, I come and I will dwell in your midst, declares the LORD."

Romans 15:9—"Therefore I will praise you among the Gentiles, and sing to your name."

1 Corinthians 14:15—"What am I to do? I will pray with my spirit, but I will pray with my mind also; I will sing praise with my spirit, but I will sing with my mind also."

Hebrews 2:12—"I will tell of your name to my brothers; in the midst of the congregation I will sing your praise."

James 5:13—"Is anyone among you suffering? Let him pray. Is anyone cheerful? Let him sing praise."

Ephesians 5:19—"Addressing one another in psalms and hymns and spiritual songs, singing and making melody to the Lord with your heart."

Colossians 3:16—"Let the word of Christ dwell in you richly, teaching and admonishing one another in all wisdom, singing psalms and hymns and spiritual songs, with thankfulness in your hearts to God."

List of Hymnals

ELW   *Evangelical Lutheran Worship*
LSB   *Lutheran Service Book*
TFF   *This Far by Faith: An African-American*
                   Resource for Worship
CWS   *Christian Worship: Supplement*

For Further Reading

> Bell, John L. *The Singing Thing: A Case for Congregational Song.* GIA Publications, 2000.

A shorter read that gets to the heart behind the human voice. Essential to understanding what motivates people to sing—and how best to enable them. Of particular importance is Bell's examination of how music forms the faith of children and the impact that has on their adult lives. Understanding such is key to renewing voices—and to repairing damage souls may have suffered in their childhoods.

> Bradley, C. Randall. *From Postlude to Prelude: Music Ministry's Other Six Days.* MorningStar Music Publishers, 2004.

Forwarded by John Whitlivet, Bradley here offers a detailed, practical guide for the church musician, whose vocation calls for musical excellence, strong organizational skills, and, above all, sensitivity to the care of souls. Many practical tips are offered in all three areas. The insights into approaching and resolving conflicts are particularly valuable.

> Byars, Roland P. *The Future of Protestant Worship: Beyond the Worship Wars.* Westminster John Knox Press, 2002.

Byars asks crucial questions that challenge many presuppositions and definitions, pointing the reader to strive for a new paradigm that is both ancient and missional: authentic worship that is "neither Contemporary nor Traditional."

> Causey, C. Harry. *Things They Didn't Tell Me: About Being a Minister of Music.* Music Revelation, 1988.

This volume from the 1980s may appear dated at first, but the lessons readily translate to our own time. A Presbyterian pastor and noted choir director, Causey outlines how cantors need the skills of politicians, financial planners, psychologists, administrators, producers, and scholars. Short chapters drawn from personal experience offer authoritative illustrations as to what it takes to flourish in music ministry.

> Clark, Linda J. *Music in Churches: Nourishing Your Congregation's Musical Life.* The Alban Institute, 1994.

Based on considerable fieldwork in congregations, this short volume uncovers the patterns and intuitions of all the participants in worship, examining the critical relationships between pastors, music directors, choir members, lay leaders, and the quieter folks hidden in the pews. Solid research on congregational attitudes toward singing is included, with helpful sample questionnaires added in the appendices. These questions are readily adapted for various contexts and should be helpful for all seeking greater coherence in worship.

> Dawn, Marva J. *A Royal "Waste" of Time: The Splendor of Worshiping God and Being Church for the World*. Eerdmans, 1999.

Beginning with a sermon for church musicians on Colossians 3:12–17 and concluding with "asking new and old questions as we remember the future," Dawn helps Christians remember their love of the Lord and gives us courage to bask in it for the sake of the world God so loved. The chapter on planning criteria includes fifteen questions pastors and musicians should consider as they work together to lead God's people in holy song.

> Eskew, Harry, and Hugh T. McElrath.
> *Sing with Understanding.* Second Edition,
> Revised and Expanded. Church Street
> Press, 1995.

A solid, accessible introduction to the study of
hymns, and a valuable retrospective for the seasoned hymnologist. The sound scholarship here
addresses hymns as literature, music, and theology,
reviews the treasury of hymn traditions we inherit
today, and discusses the effective use of hymns in
proclamation, education, worship, and ministry.
Particularly recommended for those seeking to
develop a core list of hymns for their congregation.

> Frankforter, A. Daniel. *Stones for Bread:*
> *A Critique of Contemporary Worship.*
> Westminster John Knox Press, 2001.

A robust analysis well-grounded in Scripture that
helps the reader understand the inauthenticities
promoted in the name of worship styles, both
contemporary and traditional. Frankforter uses
his skills as an historian to help the reader grasp
what communities have lost—and what idols have
been enthroned—as congregations jettisoned their
common song, and to provide good paradigms for

them to consider how best to move forward in faith.

> Funk, Virgil, ed. *Sung Liturgy Toward 2000 AD*. The Pastoral Press, 1991.

These essays from a Roman Catholic perspective proved prescient as they considered the future of congregational song in view of emerging post-modern trends. Thirty years later, one can see how much indeed transpired as a result of these social and religious currents and consider how well one's own congregation has adapted to these shifts.

> Getty, Keith, and Kristyn Getty. *Sing! How Worship Transforms Your Life, Family, and Church*. B&H Books, 2017.

This invaluable little book addresses each of the participants in planning, leading, and participating in worship—including those hugely important but often neglected members of the worship team, the sound crew. Written with great care for the souls of each participant, devotional encouragement and comfort are given in each chapter as the reader is led to key questions they should consider as they fulfill their roles in the body of Christ.

> Herl, Joseph. *Worship Wars in Early
> Lutheranism: Choir, Congregation, and
> Three Centuries of Conflict.* Oxford, 2004.

Definitely not just for Lutherans and liturgical scholars, this authoritative work dispels many myths about worship during and after the Reformation and chronicles how Lutherans gained the reputation of being "the singing church." Parallel developments among the Roman Catholic and Reformed are discussed, with attention to the people, events, and ideas that guided actual worship practice.

> Hustad, Donald P. *Jubilate II: Church
> Music in Worship and Renewal.* Hope,
> 1993.

A thorough history of evangelical worship that raises important, enduring questions for church musicians in all Christian traditions. This scholarly treatise covers the art of music, its history, and its applications with enjoyable prose. Hustad writes lovingly and honestly, with the humility that accompanies wisdom.

> *Living Voice of the Gospel: Dimensions in Wholeness for the Church Musician.* CPH, 1996.

A collection of devotional essays for the church musician. Here is not a practical guide but comfort, affirmation, and encouragement for cantors to embrace all the dimensions of their calling: creative, pastoral, historic, ecclesiastical, and theological.

> Long, Thomas G. *Beyond the Worship Wars: Building Vital and Faithful Worship.* The Alban Institute, 2001.

Starting with an honest discussion of people's motivations in worship, Long thoughtfully addresses the challenge of music in our increasingly diverse culture. Using dance as an analogy, he helpfully underscores how memory and leadership can enable a congregation to move beyond unsatisfying compromises and rejoice together in the Spirit on the Lord's Day.

➤ Mitchell, Robert H. *I Don't Like That Music.* Hope Publishing Company, 1993.

Coming from a free church perspective, where more are theoretically open to change, Mitchell underscores the intrinsic conservatism of Christian assemblies, pastorally addresses a number of common complaints about music, and offers wise guidance for introducing changes in worship.

➤ *Not Unto Us: A Celebration of the Ministry of Kurt J. Eggert.* Northwestern Publishing House, 2001.

A collection of essays in honor of a sainted and highly-esteemed musician of the Wisconsin Evangelical Lutheran Synod (WELS), the first seventy-nine pages are highlights from the many sensitive, pastoral essays from Eggert's own pen. Several chapters would be of interest mostly to those who work on hymnals and those within Eggert's denomination tradition, but Eggert's writing and the essays by Ralph D. Gehrke and Carl F. Schalk provide insights for all.

> Westermeyer, Paul. *The Church Musician.*
> Revised Edition. Augsburg Fortress, 1997.

A thoughtful analysis of the vocation of church music from a scholar who is both a pastor and a musician. Grounded in the idea of the cantor as leader of the assembly's song, proper emphasis is placed on cultivating the congregation's voice. Westermeyer also sees the cantor at the intersection of theology, liturgy, and music, and guides the reader into greater appreciation of the Lord's song and those who lead us in singing it.

> Westermeyer, Paul. *Te Deum: The Church and Music.* Fortress Press, 1998.

An essential survey of the roots of Protestant church music, beginning with worship in biblical times, continuing with the early church, and proceeding through the Reformation to today. Valuable history from the Middle Ages is included, with the resulting scope allowing the reader to consider broad questions believers have faced throughout the centuries, including the roles of psalmody, accompaniment, and even silence.

Notes

1. Robert Lowry (1826–1899), *ELW* #763.

2. Keith Getty and Kristyn Getty, *Sing! How Worship Transforms Your Life, Family, and Church* (B&H Books, 2017), 85–91.

3. Peter Pesic, director of the Science Institute at St. John's College, has done considerable work in this area. A pianist and physicist, he has written six books and many articles on the history and philosophy of science and music. A good overview is found here: Peter Pesic, "Music and the Making of Modern Science," Popular Astronomy, https://popularastronomy .technicacuriosa.com/2017/03/10/music- and-the-making-of-modern-science/.

4. Karl Paulnack, "Essay by Karl Paulnack," Janet Hammer, https://www.janethammer.com/ karl-paulnack-speech.html.

5. Nicolaus Herman (c. 1480–1561), "Let All Together Praise Our God," trans. F. Samuel Janzow, *LSB* #389, stanzas 3–5.

6. Aurelius Prudentius Clemens (348–c. 413), *LSB* 384.

7. Translation of Luke 1:74–75 from the International Commission on English in the Liturgy Corporation (ICEL), "Gospel Canticle of Zechariah (Luke 1:68–79)."

8. *LSB* #387.

9. Here I use the term "musics," a term used by musicologists, because I am dealing with categories and aspects of song that transcend stylistic boundaries.

10. A. L. Barry, *The Unchanging Feast: The Nature and Basis of Lutheran Worship* (Lutheran Church—Missouri Synod, 1995), 1.

11. *LSB* #466.

12. *LSB* #853.

13. "I Love to Tell the Story," a hymn by Kate Hankey, 1866, with refrain added by William G. Fischer, 1869, is published in 1,122 hymnals. It sings about loving to tell the story without actually telling it.

14. Harold Senkbeil, *The Care of Souls: Cultivating a Pastor's Heart* (Lexham Press, 2019), 11.

15. Senkbeil, *The Care of Souls*, 12.

16. Gene Edward Veith, "Religion, Culture, and Our Worship," *Concordia Theological Quarterly* 62.1 (1998): 31–35.

17. The author heard Fr. Michael Joncas make this point persuasively in his keynote address to the annual Lectures in Church Music held at Concordia University Chicago on October 24, 1994.

18. Phillip Magness, keynote address, Institute on Liturgy, Preaching, and Church Music, Concordia University Nebraska, July 22–25, 2008.

19. *LSB* #389.

20. "Oh, That I Had a Thousand Voices," *LSB* #811.

21. Peter Zizzo, Ric Wake, and Celine Dion, "Don't Save It All for Christmas Day" (Pez Music, 1998).

22. G. K. Chesterton, *Collected Works of G. K. Chesterton*, vol. 33, *The Illustrated London News, 1923–1925* (Ignatius, 1990), 318, emphasis added.

23. A through-composed setting is one where there is no paraphrasing of the text to fit a melody. Instead, a melody is composed that fits the text. The music is made to fit the words rather than words adapted to fit music. These settings are intrinsically more difficult to learn as they inherently have less repetition and more variety.

24. The setting of Evening Prayer we were singing is found in *LSB* 243.

25. "Lining out" is the simple practice of singing one line of a song and then having the folks sing it back.

26. Augustine of Hippo, *Confessions* (Sheed & Ward, 1942), Book IX.

27. *ELW* #607.

28. Stephen R. Johnson, "Luxuriant Lutheranism— the Organ on a Pedestal," *Fine Tuning* (blog), November 9, 2009, https://liturgysolutions .blogspot.com/2009/11/luxuriant-lutheranism-organ-on-pedestal.html.

29. Gustav Wingren, *Luther on Vocation*, trans. Carl C. Rasmussen (Wipf and Stock, 2004), 10.

30. Jaroslav Pelikan, *The Vindication of Tradition: The 1983 Jefferson Lecture in the Humanities* (Yale University Press, 1984), 65.

31. Senkbeil, *The Care of Souls*, 18.

32. *LSB* #895.

33. *LSB* #656.

34. *LSB* #507.

35. *LSB* #461.

36. From *LSB*, "Divine Service, Setting Three," 184. This liturgy is a setting of what is known among Lutherans as "The Common Service" and is the most common anglophone Lutheran order of the Communion service.

37. Marva J. Dawn, *A Royal "Waste" of Time: The Splendor of Worshiping God and Being Church for the World* (Eerdmans, 1999), 307.

38. *LSB* #357.

39. *LSB* #656.

40. *LSB* #507.

41. *LSB* #733.

42. *TFF* #77.

43. *LSB* #502.

44. *CWS* #752.

45. Getty and Getty, *Sing!*, xix–xx.

46. *LSB* #712.

47. *LSB* #483.

48. *LSB* #344.

49. *LSB* #379.

50. Mike Salvino, "How A Former Accenture CEO Turned A Failing Leadership Into Growth," Chief Executive, https://chiefexecutive.net/how-a-former-accenture-ceo-turned-a-failing-leadership-into-growth/.

51. Robert Robinson (1735–1790), "Come, Thou Fount of Every Blessing," *LSB* #686. This American standard hymn refers to 1 Sam 7:12, as the name given to the stone of remembrance raised to God's glory was named Ebenezer— which means "Thus far has the LORD helped us."

52. Sanctus Augustinus, *Enarratio in Psalmum* 72, 1: CCL 39, 986 (PL 36, 914).

53. Written by Samuel Rodigast (1649–1708), *LSB* #60.

54. Preface to the Babst Hymnal (1545), *D. Martin Luthers Werke: kritische Gesamtausgabe*, vol. 35 (Weimar: Hermann Böhlaus Nachfolger, 1923), 477:4–12; compare *Luther's Works*, vol. 53, *Word and Sacrament,* ed. E. Theodore Bachmann (Fortress, 1965), 333.

55. *LSB* #669.

56. *LSB* #555.

57. *LSB* #648.

58. This analogy, often credited to Thelonious Monk, has been used in various forms by numerous artist and entertainers and is of unknown origin. An early variation appeared in 1918 ("The Unseen World," *The New Republic*, vol. 14, p. 63)

and, in its current form, became associated with Elvis Costello (White, Timothy [October 1983]. "Elvis Costello: A Man Out of Time Beats the Clock," *Musician*, No. 60. p. 52).

59. A through-composed setting is one where there is no paraphrasing of the text to fit a melody. Instead, a melody is composed that fits the text. The music is made to fit the words rather than words adapted to fit music. These settings are intrinsically more difficult to learn as they inherently have less repetition and more variety.

Works Cited

Augustine of Hippo. *Confessions*. Sheed & Ward, 1942.

Bachmann, E. Theodore, ed. *Luther's Works*. Vol. 53, *Word and Sacrament*. Fortress, 1965.

Barry, A. L. *The Unchanging Feast: The Nature and Basis of Lutheran Worship*. Lutheran Church—Missouri Synod, 1995.

Chesterton, G. K. *Collected Works of G. K. Chesterton*. Vol. 33, *The Illustrated London News, 1923–1925*. Ignatius, 1990.

Christian Worship: Supplement. Northwestern Publishing, 2008.

Dawn, Marva J. *A Royal "Waste" of Time: The Splendor of Worshiping God and Being Church for the World*. Eerdmans, 1999.

Evangelical Lutheran Worship. Augsburg Fortress, 2006.

Getty, Keith, and Kristyn Getty. *Sing! How Worship Transforms Your Life, Family, and Church*. B&H Books, 2017.

Johnson, Stephen R. "Luxuriant Lutheranism—the Organ on a Pedestal." *Fine Tuning* (blog). November 9, 2009. https://liturgysolutions. blogspot.com/2009/11/luxuriant-lutheranism-organ-on-pedestal.html.

Luther, Martin. *D. Martin Luthers Werke: kritische Gesamtausgabe*. Vol. 35. Weimar: Hermann Böhlaus Nachfolger, 1923.

Lutheran Service Book. Concordia Publishing House, 2005.

Magness, Phillip. Keynote address. Institute on Liturgy, Preaching, and Church Music, 2008.

Paulnack, Karl. "Essay by Karl Paulnack." Janet Hammer. https://www.janethammer.com/karl-paulnack-speech.html.

Pelikan, Jaroslav. *The Vindication of Tradition: The 1983 Jefferson Lecture in the Humanities*. Yale University Press, 1984.

Pesic, Peter. "Music and the Making of Modern Science." *Popular Astronomy*. March 10, 2017. https://popularastronomy.technicacuriosa.com/2017/03/10/music-and-the-making-of-modern-science/.

Salvino, Mike. "How A Former Accenture CEO Turned A Failing Leadership Into Growth." Chief Executive. https://chiefexecutive.net/how-a-former-accenture-ceo-turned-a-failing-leadership-into-growth/.

Senkbeil, Harold L. *The Care of Souls: Cultivating a Pastor's Heart*. Lexham Press, 2019.

This Far by Faith: An African-American Resource for Worship. Augsburg, 1999.

Veith, Gene Edward. *Postmodern Times: A Christian Guide to Contemporary Thought and Culture.* Crossway, 1994.

Wingren, Gustav. *Luther on Vocation.* Translated by Carl C. Rasmussen. Wipf and Stock, 2004.

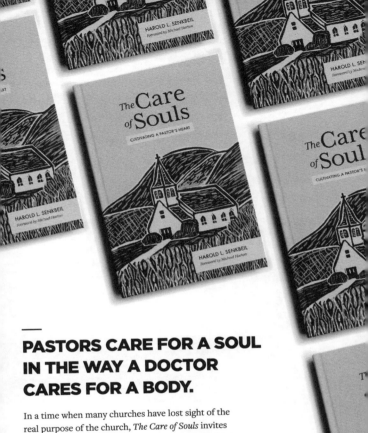

PASTORS CARE FOR A SOUL IN THE WAY A DOCTOR CARES FOR A BODY.

In a time when many churches have lost sight of the real purpose of the church, *The Care of Souls* invites a new generation of pastors to form the godly habits and practical wisdom needed to minister to the hearts and souls of those committed to their care.

"Pastoral theology at its best. Every pastor, and everyone who wants to be a pastor, should read this book."
—Timothy George, Founding Dean, Beeson Divinity School, Samford University; General Editor, Reformation Commentary on Scripture